FOF

SHORT TAKES ON LIFE

PETER LAWRENCE

ISBN: 9781691719419

Questions

Question 1: When is the best time to do each thing?

Question 2: Who are the most important people at any time?

Question 3: What is the most important thing to do at all times?

Question 4: What gives you more joy, being loved by someone or loving someone?

Question 5: A mother and daughter are in a car crash that kills the mom. The daughter is rushed to the hospital. The emergency room nurse looks at the girl and exclaims, "This girl is my daughter!" How is this possible?

Question 6: One day you are kidnapped and you wake up in a sealed hotel room, where food is delivered through a trapdoor. While watching the television, you learn that your spouse has been murdered and you are the prime suspect. You are unable to figure out who could have done this to you and why. You plan and attempt to escape but without any success. Fifteen years pass by, and one day you are sedated and you wake up on a roof-top. You feel liberated and you go on living. Time goes by, and you finally meet the person responsible for your captivity all those years. What will be your first question to the kidnapper?

The answers to these questions and more are revealed in this book. To get the most out of this book, please read it sequentially, instead of jumping around or skimming.

Random Ramblings

Faith

When we say we have faith in something, chances are it is not an absolute faith. It is faith contingent upon several factors that we are not even aware of until that faith is tested.

In June 1859, Jean-François Gravelet, also known as Charles Blondin, the famous French tightrope walker, attempted to become the first person to cross a tightrope stretched over Niagara Falls. He walked across the Falls several times, each time performing a more challenging feat, including crossing while blindfolded. Finally, he asked the crowd, "Do you believe I can carry a person across the Falls in this wheelbarrow?" The crowd enthusiastically shouted, "Yes!" By that time, they had come to believe he was the greatest tightrope walker in the world, and that he could do anything.

Now, let me ask you: Do you have faith in his capability?

Blondin asked for volunteers and the crowd went silent. Nobody wanted to get in the wheelbarrow. Just a moment ago, they believed he could do anything! Would you have volunteered to get in Blondin's wheelbarrow if you were there? What happened to faith in his powers? Later that year, his manager Harry Colcord did ride on Blondin's back across the Falls, becoming the first person to ride on someone's back across the Niagara Falls.

It is nice to have friends like Harry Colcord who trust you with their lives.

Success

Whose life meant more?

Person A's life had a positive impact on ten people.

Person B's life had a positive impact on one person.

Consider the following now:

The ten people that person A impacted did not go on to positively impact any other lives. The one person that person B impacted went on to positively impact hundreds of lives, generation after generation. Now, whose life meant more, person A or person B?

The full impact a person has on others may go beyond our time and space, hence the futility of comparing or judging.

Leslie Cheung was a film actor and musician from Hong Kong. Cheung was considered one of the founding fathers of Cantopop. He was rich, famous and envied by many. On April Fool's Day 2003, he leaped from the 24th floor of the Mandarin Oriental hotel in Hong Kong. He left a suicide note saying that he had been suffering from depression. I am told that the hotel's windows are not easily opened. And yet, he was so determined to take his life that he took the time and effort to open the window and jump out.

John Kennedy Toole never got to publish his book *A Confederacy of Dunces* because no one expressed interest in it, including Simon and Schuster. Eleven years after John committed suicide, his mother, with the help of Walker Percy, got the book published. Toole was posthumously awarded the Pulitzer Prize for Fiction, and the novel is now considered a canonical work of modern literature of the Southern United States.

Cicero refused the high government position that Caesar offered him, opting for retirement instead. During retirement, he embarked on a search for truth, which culminated in *De Officiis,* which means "On Duties" or "On Obligations."

Charles M. Schwab was president of one of the world's largest steel companies. He became very wealthy. Nevertheless, he died bankrupt.

Which of the above people do you consider a success? To his generation, Cicero was considered a failure. Today, some will argue that Cicero was a success because he was true to himself. We all have a tendency to prematurely judge ourselves and others based on the past or present, not knowing what the future holds. A Chinese proverb has the following advice: "Do not judge a man until his coffin is closed."

God judges us only at the end of time, and yet we mortals are so quick to pass judgments.

Good luck, bad luck

There is a parable of an old man who had one son and one horse. One day, his horse runs away.

The old man's friends and neighbors comment, "It is just bad luck!"

The old man, while stroking his long beard, replies, "Good luck, bad luck, who knows?"

A day later, the horse returns, bringing with it other wild horses.

The old man's friends and neighbors comment, "It is just good luck!"

The old man, while stroking his long beard, replies, "Good luck, bad luck, who knows?"

A week later, while trying to tame the wild horses, the son falls and breaks his leg.

The old man's friends and neighbors comment, "It is just bad luck!"

The old man, while stroking his long beard, replies, "Good luck, bad luck, who knows?"

A month later, the army comes to the village and recruits all able young men to the army, but the old man's son is spared because of his injury.

The old man's friends and neighbors comment, "It is just good luck!"

The old man, while stroking his long beard, replies, "Good luck, bad luck, who knows?"

None of us have 20/20 foresight, and hence none of us are aware of the implications of the 'good luck' and 'bad luck' events that we experience. Try to keep the above story in mind, especially when undergoing one setback after another. One's attitude and time can be alchemists, transforming the curses of today to blessings tomorrow. When things go well, it serves us well to be grateful, but not to get too elated. With practice, hopefully, we can reach a state of equanimity such that under any circumstances, like the old man, we can say, "Good luck, bad luck, who knows?" Stroking of beard is optional.

"When love and hatred cannot affect you,
Profit and loss cannot touch you,
Praise and blame cannot ruffle you,
You are honored by all the world" (Lao Tzu)

Greyhound

At the greyhound races, as soon as the doors open, the greyhounds charge off at speeds over 40 mph. They chase after a rabbit with such gusto. But why? Would they still give their all if they knew the race was rigged so they could never catch the rabbit? Or that even if they somehow caught it, it is fake? It is merely a mechanical rabbit. Is whatever that is dangled before you, which you are chasing with all your time and energy, real and worth pursuing? Is there any way to be certain of it? You do not want to spend your entire life on a pursuit, only to find toward the end of your life that it was all futile. When your coffin finally closes, what will all that you struggled and toiled for mean? Were all the anger, anxieties, frustrations and bickering worth it? What survives your death? Among these, which deserves your lifelong toil?

Carrot and the stick

Imagine that you tie a stick to the harness of a donkey, such that it extends above and in front of the animal's head. Now tie a carrot at the end of the stick, such that it is just out of reach of the donkey's mouth. The donkey, motivated by the dangling carrot, moves forward to take a bite, but because the carrot is attached to the stick and the stick to the harness, the carrot too moves forward and remains out of reach, eternally. The donkey keeps moving, and perhaps may even be more motivated with each step as it burns up its energy, wanting the carrot even more. You can saddle the donkey with any burden, and as long as a carrot is dangling in front of it, it keeps moving, believing that the prize is just ahead. It is possible that if this keeps going, the poor donkey may collapse from exhaustion. Sometimes, the donkey is a human, and the Japanese have a word for death from overwork – *Karōshi.*

Looking for a challenge?

Forget about running a marathon, taking part in a triathlon, or climbing Mount Everest. I bet there is no greater challenge than trying to love your neighbor as yourself! Imagine the world of tomorrow, if mankind can undertake this challenge and succeed…

Love

"What gives you more joy, being loved by someone or loving someone?" a friend once asked me. He went on to say that *all* our joy comes from the latter. Most people will disagree, and if you are in the 'most' category, consider the following:

You are being loved by someone, but you are unaware of it. Do you get any joy at all?

You love a person deeply, but that person is unaware of it. At that point, doesn't *all* your joy come just from loving the person, irrespective of whether it is requited or not?

It is wonderful to be in a position where you crave love from none, yet give love to all. If you are still unconvinced that *all* your joy can come from loving, please continue to mull it over. Hopefully, by the end of this book, a dialog between two characters may change your thinking.

Fulfillment

Sometimes, some people can keep eating and yet continue to feel hungry. Gorging oneself with empty calories is no substitute for the essential nutrients that the body needs. Eating a variety of different colors of fruits and vegetables together with nuts, grains and legumes can provide the necessary nutrients that the body needs, such that one can cut down on the calories without experiencing hunger. Calorie restriction is a proven way to slow the aging process and maintain peak vitality. The goal, then, should be to consume nutrition-dense food rather than calorie-rich foods. Unfortunately, many people choose the latter. And when they continue to feel hungry, they continue to stuff themselves with the same junk, with processed or packaged foods. But no amount of foods rich in energy, but poor in nutrition, will fulfill the body's craving. Likewise, no amount of material stuff can fulfill our highest needs.

In 1943, Abraham Maslow put forth his theory of human motivation, commonly known as Maslow's Hierarchy of Needs. At the bottom of the pyramid are the physiological needs. At the apex is the need for self-actualization. In the developed world, despite having easily fulfilled their lower-level needs, many do not seem fulfilled. The reason is they are trying to satisfy their highest need with lower-level stuff. The pursuit to keep up and beat the Joneses is deemed as the ultimate success.

As such, they continue to play in the lower levels of the pyramid instead of recognizing that they have enough and transcending to higher levels of the pyramid. As long as you are stuck in the mode that you have to have a bigger house, a faster car, etc; you are never going to be fully satisfied. Just as your body's needs cannot be satisfied with empty calories, your soul's cravings cannot be satisfied by material stuff either. As Abraham Maslow said, "A musician must make music, an artist must paint, a poet must write if he is to be ultimately at peace with himself."

Inspiration

Michelangelo said: "I saw an angel in the block of marble and I just chiseled until I set him free." That is inspiration. That is what should move us to work. Not work for the sake of work. Different people find inspiration in different things. Michelangelo found his in marble. Where do you find yours?

Focus on your strength

"Running a marathon at a world-class speed, say 2:12 for men, is a feat that most people are going to find is impossible, because their bodies are just not biomechanically designed to be able to achieve that result. No matter how hard they train, no matter how determined, no matter what their emotional strength is, they are not going to be able to achieve that type of a standard, because it is just physically impossible. They may run a marathon, and they may even run it in reasonably good time, but they will not run in it in a world-class time. A few people will be able to do it, because physically they have the right type of body. It has to be a combination of both the physical capability and the determination and hard work." (Mr. Jack Schwager)

Sir John Templeton wanted to be a missionary but discovered he did not have the health and stamina. He was good at investment though, and thought maybe he could serve the church by focusing on his strength. He became a pioneer in global investment.

The Amazon jungle is full of huge, fast or poisonous creatures. Examples include jaguars, bullet ants, and poison dart frogs. But the peaceful sloth is also a resident there. It ranks very low when it comes to the sense of taste, touch, sight, hearing, and, of course, speed. So how does it survive? The answer: By being true to its nature - by being very slow! Its long hours of sleep keeps it from being noticed by predators. It blends in with its surroundings because its hairs shelter algae that are brown during the dry season and green during the wet season. Scientists are discovering that some species of fungi found in sloth fur could eventually be a potent force against certain parasites, cancers, and bacteria. It was the very lack of speed of the sloth that allowed its fur to be a conducive environment for these fungi.

Imagine if the sloth had yielded to peer pressure and mustered all its energy, and picked up speed. Okay, perhaps it wouldn't be as swift as a jaguar, but suppose it became fast enough that it was no longer a cozy home for the fungi. Wouldn't that be a loss to society? Scientists did not know about the value of the sloth or the fungi until recently. Likewise, society might not come to appreciate someone or something until years later. Sometimes, we may not recognize our value. But neither does the sloth know that it is harboring microorganisms, or that some of these microorganisms will serve to benefit mankind down the road.

We have a tendency to undervalue what we have because it comes to us effortlessly. But what comes to you easily is what may be needed. Crowds tend to be wise only if individual members act responsibly and make their own decisions based on their circle of competence, unadulterated by the influence of a group or authority.

The nuclear submarine
USS Scorpion mysteriously disappeared on May 22nd, 1968. The only possible solution, one might have thought, was to track down three or four top experts on submarines and ocean currents, ask them where they thought the Scorpion was, and search there. Naval

officer John Craven had a different plan. He assembled a team of men with a wide range of knowledge, including mathematicians, submarine specialists, and salvage men. Instead of asking them to consult with each other to come up with an answer, he asked each of them to offer his best guess. He took all the guesses, and used a formula to estimate the Scorpion's final location. Five months after the Scorpion disappeared, a Navy ship found it. It was 220 yards from where Craven's group had said it would be. No one person in the group was right, but their composite estimate was in the ballpark, because every person in the group, including Craven, stayed true to their respective expertise.

One of the remaining survivors of the 1906 San Francisco earthquake is Winnie Hook. On Valentine's Day in 2012, she celebrated her 106th birthday. She lives in the same city as I did – Santa Clara, and I had the pleasure of congratulating her on her birthday. According to her, one of the advantages of living that long is, "There is no peer pressure."

You do not have to outlive everyone to live without peer pressure. You can do so today by dancing to the beat of your heart instead of to that of others. Focus on your strength.

Caffeine crash

If you take a knife and cut your wrist you will bleed. The consequence of any action is embodied within the action. While some consequences are visible immediately, others are more subtle, delayed, or cumulative. And it is the actions with subtle, delayed, or cumulative consequences that seduce people to engage in activities they should not. What begins as an exception eventually becomes a habit, since they think they are committing it with impunity. The day of reckoning comes, if not now, eventually

There is a story of a man who jumped off the roof of a building. As he passed each floor, the people inside the building could hear him say, "So far so good... so far so good..."

You may have come across people who earn about the same as you or even less, but are living a life that is more luxurious than yours. They usually achieve this by taking on debt, which means they are spending their future paychecks now. Some people achieve some ‘abnormal’ physical capabilities in the short term, like the ability to go without sleep, or exceptional endurance. Again, most of the time, these feats are not sustainable, because they are just ‘spending it forward’. And while they are spending it, yes, “so far so good.” But inevitably, just like the man falling off the building, they will face the inevitable crash.

When a person is tired, the brain produces adenosine. To keep working, one may resort to several cups of coffee. The caffeine in the coffee blocks the adenosine, and the person experiences a temporary boost in energy. But the brain continues to produce adenosine. Eventually the caffeine wears off, and the adenosine that has been building up overwhelms your brain's receptors, and you experience the crash.

Long term thinking

Could you imagine starting a project that you know you will not finish in ten, twenty, or even thirty years? Now, imagine starting a project that you won't even see completed in your grandchildren's lifetime. Will you begin such a project? The Cologne Cathedral is a testament to what is possible with a vision. Construction work has been going on for about 800 years, including a 300-year break in between.

Life has a processional effect. Everything in life is cumulative. Turing built on Gödel's work and laid the foundation for computer science. Isaac Newton's accomplishments in mathematics and physics laid the foundations for modern science. Newton benefited from Galileo, and Galileo, in turn, was influenced by Copernicus.

Go ahead and plant the seed, even if you may not benefit from its fruits.

The Power of waiting

In an age of instant gratification, waiting is deemed as unacceptable and unproductive. However, there are merits in purposeful waiting. In the book *Siddhartha* by Hermann Hesse, the protagonist is extremely proud of his ability to do three things, one of which is to wait. The "marshmallow experiment" conducted by the psychologist Walter Mischel suggests that those who had the ability to wait for the second marshmallow generally grew up to be better in several areas compared to their peers who were unable to wait. In fact, this ability to wait is an even better predictor of college entrance exam scores than IQ scores.

There are three ways one can finance their needs and wants: credit, savings or passive income.

Credit: Those who finance their purchases by credit are similar to the children who grabbed the available marshmallow, thus forfeiting the second marshmallow. The four-year-olds who did not have the power to wait for twenty minutes or so lost the opportunity to get the second marshmallow. When I say "buying on credit," I am referring to those who do not pay the balance in full and hence incur interest charges. Those who finance their wants this way, end up paying much more for the product than what it costs. Depending on how long they prolong the payment, it is conceivable that their interest charges may match the price of the product itself. One can get into debt instantly, but paying it off may take years.

Savings: If one has the ability to wait until one has sufficient savings to buy it outright, then the person saves on the interest payments. Though this method of financing is better than the earlier method, this is still not the best way to finance your purchases. It is not the best way because when you use your savings, you are using up your principal. The principal which is the seed that has the potential to yield passive income.

Passive Income: Passive income is any income that is generated by you not having to work. Instead of you working, your savings are working hard for you, such that they generate the income. Very few people achieve this mode of financing their purchases because this can only be achieved by people who have the ability to wait long enough. The ability to wait until the savings, assets or investments generates sufficient passive income to fund whatever they need to purchase. In this mode of financing, the person is not giving up his principal. The principal is preserved and continue to generate income. People in this group are similar to the group of children that were able to wait to earn the second marshmallow. They did not work any harder to earn the second marshmallow. Like Siddhartha, all they possessed was the ability to wait. The power of compounding is enjoyed by those who wait. Those unable to wait for their financial resources to grow over time are usually tempted into get-rich-quick schemes.

The power of waiting is not only visible in the growth of your nest egg, but it eventually leads to reduced wants too. You see, if you wait long enough, your transient desires may eventually go away. Hence waiting eliminates impulsive purchases.

Grocery stores estimate that more than 50 percent of purchases are impulse purchases. When it comes to anything in fashion, if you wait, what is fashionable now will eventually become out of fashion. At that point, you will no longer be incented to make the purchase. If it is electronics stuff, waiting rewards you with a better value for money. Is it cheaper to buy a smartphone when it first comes out, or months later?

When I was young, I did not get much chance to go to the cinema, because we couldn't afford it. I remember one weekend, on my way to the school for some extracurricular activities; I noticed a very long line queuing up to buy the tickets for the latest James Bond movie, *Moonraker*. Later that week, I will hear from many people how spectacular the movie was. Years later, when I was serving in the army, that movie was screened for free at the army barracks. While watching the movie, I could not help chuckling and asking - this was what the excitement was all about, back then? I am sure if I had watched it when it first came out; I will have been "blown away" too. But isn't that the way with all stuff? So, the next time you are tempted to jump on the bandwagon or join the long queue to be one of the first to purchase the latest and greatest, remember that this craze will pass too. Realizing that will make it easier for you to wait. And as I suggested earlier, if you wait, your desire for whatever you wanted may fade too, especially if it is a fad. If you really cannot wait to get something, ask yourself: How did I survive all this while without it?

As more and more of your impulsive and wasteful wants get eradicated, the less passive income is needed to finance your calibrated wants. You are also allowing the passive income to compound instead of raiding it. When your passive income matches or exceeds your total expenses needed to finance your needs and wants, you achieve financial independence.

With any worthwhile pursuits, if you are thinking of quitting, wait to quit; after all, you can always quit later. If you wait long enough, you will reap the asymmetrical reward reserved only for the last person standing.

People

Ronald Reagan said: "Government is not a solution to our problem, government is the problem." Abraham Lincoln, on the other hand, envisioned "Government of the people, by the people, for the people." Hmm! According to Reagan, government is the problem, but per Lincoln, the government is formed by people … so aren't people the problem?

Some may argue that the government is no longer as Lincoln envisioned. They say it is currently "Government of the corporation, by the corporation, for the corporation." But aren't corporations people too? At least, that's what the U.S. Supreme Court decided. Even if you choose to disagree with the U.S. Supreme Court; you can't disagree that people form corporations. The CEOs of corporations are people, so are the board of directors of a corporation. When a CEO lays off people (employees), the stock price of the company usually goes up. Why is that? People (shareholders) suddenly find the company more worthwhile when fellow people are fired. So whether it is the government or the corporation or society as a whole, the building blocks of these are people. If the government or corporation is undesirable, isn't it because the majority of the people are undesirable? Isn't the government or corporation a reflection of the people it is made of? So if we are not happy with what we see, the change should start with each of the building blocks. And when there are sufficient numbers, or when it reaches a tipping point, we would see the change we desire. We must be the change we wish to see in the world. Change begins with each of us, we the people, wanting to change.

Even if we recognize the need to change, do we honestly know what sort of change we want and the best way to achieve it? How can we ensure that the actions we the people take do not take us out of the frying pan and into the fire?

Eisenhower, in his farewell address, stressed the importance of an alert and knowledgeable citizenry. Is knowledge alone enough? Weapons of mass destructions were created by knowledgeable citizenry. The financial meltdown was created by knowledgeable citizenry. Highly-educated people came up with collateralized debt obligations (CDOs) and credit default swaps (CDS). Mathematics whiz kids came up with models to assign risk. But look at what happened. Clearly, knowledge itself is not sufficient.

The Quintessential question

If you could ask for anything in this world, what would you ask for?

Take a moment to think and write down your answer.

When God offered King Solomon the opportunity to ask for whatever he wanted, Solomon asked for wisdom. If you have wisdom, you should be able to get anything else using wisdom. Without wisdom, even if you are fortunate enough to have your dreams come true, you will either abuse it or eventually lose it. Recall the proverb "A fool and his money are soon parted." Statistics on lottery winners validate this. Be it wealth, health or whatever; without wisdom, we will not judiciously manage whatever we have.

Is wisdom alone sufficient? What about fortitude? Wisdom helps us distinguish between right and wrong. Fortitude gives us the courage to make the right decision and stand by it irrespective of its repercussions. Many people during Nazi Germany had some inkling that something was not right. However, they either did not have the fortitude to dig deeper or were unable to muster the courage to defy authority. Regrettably, this is true even today. The Milgram experiment, which has been repeated several times over the years and across several cultures, always arrives at the same conclusion: Most people succumb to authority, even though their conscience tells them otherwise.

Practice can be one way to develop fortitude. Even seemingly insignificant acts of courage done often will aid in building our spine to face a major crisis down the road. In his book, *Outliers*, Malcolm Gladwell mentions the 10,000-hour rule. According to him, practicing a specific task for 10,000 hours or more offers us a good chance of being successful at that task. Our daily lives present us with ample opportunities to clock in these hours. Was there a time when you knew something was not right, but you ignored your better angels because everybody was doing it? Is there anything about which you are afraid to dig deeper, because you are afraid you will uncover something you would rather not know? Excuses such as "I just followed orders" or "I did not know" or "Everybody does it" could be symptoms of cowardice. Acts of courage may not necessarily win us medals of bravery. In some cases, we may even be ostracized. But if we pass up on minute opportunities to do the right thing, do you seriously think we will have the fortitude to do the right thing when it matters most?

Fortitude sometimes implies not doing anything either. Remember the Cuban Missile Crisis? If we had a trigger-happy cowboy as the President then, he would have easily caved in and done the unthinkable. It takes fortitude to say no. It takes fortitude to exercise restraint. It takes fortitude to exhibit patience. It takes fortitude to be able to let go. None of these are easy. But the more we practice it, the better we get at it.

One person can make a difference

On September 1st, 1983, Russia shot down a Korean commercial plane. Tensions were high between the US and Russia. A few weeks later, Colonel Stanislav Petrov was in charge of an early-warning bunker outside of Moscow when the system reported that a missile had been launched from the United States, followed by up to five more. Colonel Petrov trusted his judgment that the warning was a false alarm, and he did not alert command headquarters. If he had just followed protocol, it may have set in motion an unwarranted retaliatory nuclear exchange. One person's decision saved humanity from a nuclear catastrophe.

Money

Not all aphorisms are true. Money is not the root of all evil. Money, just like technology or power is a tool, and a tool amplifies your effort. A good person will use money, technology, or power to do more good, while a bad person will utilize them to do more harm.

There is an American Indian proverb that reads as follows: "Only when the last tree is dead, the last river poisoned, and the last fish caught, you'll realize that you can't eat money". It will be a sad day if we arrive at that point, because we can have all the money in the world then, and still be impoverished. At that point, all we can do with money is to burn it to keep ourselves warm, and that apparently has happened before.

Contentment

Egyptian pyramids were tombs for the pharaohs. The pharaohs were buried together with luxurious items including pets and servants to ensure they have the same cushy life in their next life. A ridiculous ancient belief? If we cannot take our money and possessions when we die, why do some people live like they could?

Joseph Heller was the author of the book *Catch 22*. Once, at a party, his friend came to him and asked, "Joe, how does it make you feel to know that our host, only yesterday, may have made more money than your novel 'Catch-22' has earned in its entire history?"
And Joe replied, "I've got something he can never have."
Puzzled, his friend asked, "What on earth could that be, Joe?"
And Joe said, "The knowledge that I've got enough."

I guess that's the secret, right? Knowing when it is enough. Endless accumulation for something that you cannot enjoy once you are dead is pointless. There is also the diminishing marginal utility of wealth, meaning that beyond a certain point, more wealth has a correspondingly smaller increase in satisfaction and happiness. Too much is just as bad as too little. Between 1793 and 1794, countless members of the French high society were guillotined. In the 1970s, communists in Cambodia slaughtered the affluent. There is a Taoist parable about grave robbers who hammer the corpse's forehead, break his cheekbones and smash his jaws, all because the dead man was foolish enough to be buried with a pearl in his mouth. And yes, most of the pharaohs' tombs were robbed too.

Impossible?

In 2008, Lorenzo Odone died one day after his 30th birthday, but having lived 22 years longer than doctors predicted. Lorenzo was diagnosed at the age of six with adrenoleukodystrophy, or ALD, which leads to an accumulation of fatty acids that damage the myelin sheath. Lorenzo's parents, despite not having medical training, ignored the doctor's prognosis and went on to formulate an oil that would prolong their son's life. A study published in 2005, based on research involving 88 boys, showed that a treatment made from olive and rapeseed oils, patented by Lorenzo Odone's father, can prevent the onset of the symptoms for most boys diagnosed with ALD.

Michelangelo designed the dome of St Peter's Basilica in Rome when he was 72. Olga Kotelko took up track at age 77 and was still competing in track and field in her nineties. Until 1954, doctors and scientists said that running a mile under 4 minutes would kill you. After Dr. Roger Bannister proved that wrong, he said, "The main obstacle to achieving the impossible may be a self-limiting mind set."

Esperanza

Previously published on my blog post on May 12th, 2016.

Peace talks are going on between the Colombian government and the rebel group. Some Colombians don't seem supportive of it. When asked why, they say that the government is being manipulated by the rebel group, that some of the bad things that the rebel group was involved in are still going on, and that there is no justice if all these rebels do not go to prison for what they did. I try not to get involved in politics, especially when I am a foreigner and the discussion is not in a language I am fluent in. Nevertheless, I could not help offering my two cents: I asked them what the alternative was. Shouldn't they give peace a chance? I also told them that when we think of justice, we should not restrict ourselves to think only of the retributive aspect of justice. There is also the restorative aspect of justice. In restorative justice, the perpetrators request amnesty from civil and criminal prosecution in return for admission of the truth. I asked them if they knew what happened in South Africa after the abolition of apartheid, and encouraged them to read about the Truth and Reconciliation

Commission as an example of restorative justice.

What I said did not make any difference in their stance. I could not help wondering if peace was possible.

Outside of Colombia, things are not that rosy either – at least, based on headline news. Massive earthquakes in Ecuador and Japan, droughts in Venezuela and India, and global temperatures smashing previous records. Recently, the chief executive of insurance market Lloyd's of London warned that manmade risks had become bigger threats than natural disasters. Any reason to be hopeful about the future?

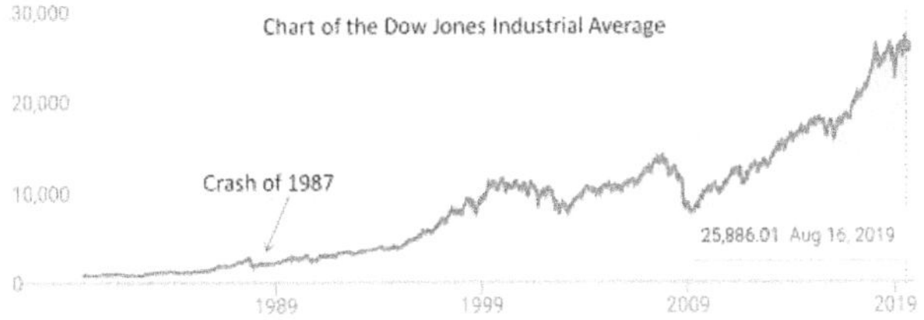

When the Crash of 1987 happened, it was a big deal, especially then. With the passage of time and looking at the above chart, you will notice at least 3 things:

1. The 1987 crash only appears as a blip.

2. Every subsequent crash appears to be of a bigger magnitude.

3. Despite the pessimism that may be prevailing aftermath of any crash, the market eventually recovers and continues on its rising trend.

Human progress is the same way. Two steps forward, one step backward. No matter how depressing things may seem, eventually mankind reverts to its path of gradual betterment. So, even if XXX becomes the next President of the U.S., and there are cyber-attacks, pandemics, and acts of terrorism – eventually, they too shall pass, and mankind will continue chugging along. It is important to have this mindset, this hope.

Decades ago, a scientist performed an experiment with some rats. He threw them into a bucket of circulating water to determine how long it took for the rats to give up and stop swimming. The average time was 15 minutes.

He then repeated the experiment with a new group of rats. But this time, he "rescued" the rats just after they had given up swimming (around 15 minutes). They were dried off, fed and allowed to recuperate before he threw them back in the bucket of water. Guess how long it took them before they gave up?

These rats were able to swim for up to 60 hours before giving up. Clearly, the earlier 15 minutes was not a physical limitation. The scientist, Curt Richter, attributed this miraculous difference to hope.

A la esperanza/To hope

Better than multitasking

Meditation is focusing continuously on one thought or action. If you are eating, just eat. If you are walking, just walk. Meditation is all about favoring one thought or activity over another. Meditation, in its most basic sense, is simply focused attention. When you focus on one thought or action, you get more out of it. Since I retired from the working life, many of my meals are eaten alone. However, I enjoy it tremendously. I prepare most of my meals, which whets my appetite and gets me salivating. When the meal is ready, I employ all my senses to enjoy the fruits of my labor. I inhale the aroma; I savor every bite as I chew mindfully. (Hard-core chewers recommend as many as fifty chews per mouthful). Hence, even though it is a very simple meal, I get more out of it because I am focused 100 percent on enjoying the task at hand - eating. Eating out with friends is a good experience too. But it is good because of the company. The time you spent with your friends will have been good even without the meal. To enjoy anything to the fullest, meditate. This means giving your entire attention to that thought or deed. So the next time you are with someone, turn the cell phone off and dedicate 100 percent of your attention to that person.

A model for daily living

You may have read Leo Tolstoy's "Three Questions." In case you have not, here is my abbreviated version.

A king was prepared to offer a huge reward to anyone who could answer three questions:

Question 1: When is the best time to do each thing?

Question 2: Who are the most important people at any time?

Question 3: What is the most important thing to do at all times?

He received varied answers from the learned men in his kingdom, but none satisfied him enough to merit the reward.

The king decided to seek the answers from a hermit known for his wisdom. The hermit was digging some garden beds in front of his hut when the king arrived. Though the hermit listened to the king's questions, the hermit continued digging without providing any answers. The king, noticing the hermit was weak and tired, offered to take over the digging.

After digging a while, the king posed the questions again. The hermit still did not answer. Later, a man ran toward them, his hands covering his stomach and blood flowing out from under them. When he reached the king, he fell to the ground, fainting.

The king and the hermit unfastened the man's clothing. There was a large wound in his stomach. The king washed it as best he could and bandaged it, but the blood would not stop flowing. The king removed the blood-soaked bandages, then repeatedly washed and re-bandaged the wound until the blood ceased to flow. With the hermit's help, the king carried the wounded man into the hut and laid him on the bed. Tired from all the work he had done, the king fell asleep. When he awoke in the morning, the man he had saved asked for forgiveness.

"I do not know you, and have nothing to forgive you for," said the king.

"You do not know me, but I know you. I am your enemy, who swore revenge against you because you executed my brother and seized my property. I knew you had gone alone to see the hermit, so I resolved to kill you on your way back. But the day passed, and you did not return. I came out from my hiding place to find you, but I came upon your bodyguards. They recognized me and wounded me. I escaped from them and would have bled to death if you had not dressed my wound. I wished to kill you, and you saved my life. Now, if I live, and if you wish it, I will serve you as your most faithful slave and will bid my sons do the same. Forgive me!"

The king was very glad to have made peace with his enemy and to have gained him as a friend. He took leave from the wounded man and approached the hermit.

"For the last time, I beg you to answer my questions, wise man," the king said.

"You have already been answered!" said the hermit.

"How answered? What do you mean?" asked the king.

"Do you not see?" replied the hermit. "If you had not pitied my weakness yesterday and had not dug these beds for me, that man would have attacked you, and you would have repented of not having stayed with me. So, the most important time was when you were digging the beds. I was the most important man; to do me good was your most important business. Afterwards, when that man ran to us, the most important time was when you were attending to him; if you had not bound up his wounds, he would have died without having made peace with you. So, he was the most important man, and what you did for him was your most important business.

Remember then: there is only one time that is important—now! It is the most important time because it is the only time when we have any power. The most important person at any time is the one who is with you, for no man knows whether he will ever have dealings with anyone else. And the most important thing is to do that person good, because for that purpose alone was man sent into this life."

Isn't this a great model for daily living?

Two monks and a beautiful woman

Two monks were traveling together. At one point, they came to a river with a strong current. As the monks were preparing to cross the river, they saw a very young and beautiful woman also attempting to cross. The young woman asked if they could help her cross to the other side.

Without hesitation, the older monk picked up the woman, carried her across the river, placed her gently on the other side, and carried on his journey.

The younger monk was stunned. An hour passed without a word between them. Two hours passed, then three, and finally the younger monk could not contain himself any longer, and blurted out "Brother, our spiritual training teaches us to avoid any contact with women, but you picked that one up and carried her!"

The older monk looked at him and replied, "Brother, I set her down on the other side of the river hours ago, why are *you* still carrying her?"

How often do we unnecessarily carry our resentment, suspicion, and self-righteousness? The younger monk allowed himself to be dictated by the letter of the law and failed to understand the spirit of the law.

The older monk exemplifies the model for daily living. He lives in the present moment, does what needs to be done, and moves on.

The importance of asking the right question

Recall question 6? The idea for the question came to me after watching a Korean movie, *Oldboy*. In that movie, a businessman named Oh Dae-su is kidnapped and goes through the ordeal mentioned in the question. Towards the end of the movie, Dae-su's captor tells him: "Ask not why you were imprisoned. Ask why you were set free."

If Dae-su had wondered why the captor had set him free instead of why he was imprisoned, his subsequent actions may have led him on a different path. The questions we ask are important.

If a person or entity can lead you to ask the wrong questions, they don't have to worry about answers that really matter. Even if you get the right answer to your question; it is useless if it is the wrong question. You don't get answers to questions you don't ask.

During World War II, the bombers that managed to return from their missions showed concentrations of bullet holes in three areas: The fuselage, the outer wings, and the tail. The recommendation, consequently, was to add armor to all of these heavily damaged areas of the plane.

But a statistician, Abraham Wald, reviewed the data and noticed a critical flaw in the analysis. They had failed to ask the right question: Where will the bullet holes be in the bombers that did not return? If a bomber made it back safely with bullet holes in the fuselage, the outer wings or the tail, it meant those bullet holes weren't fatal. They never saw bullet holes on the cockpit or the engines of the bombers that made it back. These are the vulnerable parts of the bomber, and hence where armor was needed. This finding helped to turn the tide of the war.

Truth – part 1

The Boston Globe's Joe Keohane reported that researchers at the University of Michigan found that when misinformed people, particularly political partisans, were exposed to corrected facts in news stories, they rarely changed their minds. Instead of changing their minds to reflect the correct information, they would entrench themselves even deeper.

Gayla Benefield uncovered an awful secret about her hometown that explained why its mortality rate was 80 times higher than anywhere else in the U.S. But when she tried to tell people about it, she learned an even more shocking truth: People did not want to know the truth. They were not interested to know about the toxic asbestos dust from the vermiculite mines. The company that owned the mine offered Gayla money to suppress the truth, but she refused.

This seems to be a recurring theme throughout history: One person sensing something is not right digs deeper to uncover the truth, but the masses are not initially interested in the truth, and the powerful employ various methods to suppress the truth. Truth is persecuted more by the wicked than it is loved by the good.

Eventually, the truth did prevail in Gayla's hometown, and a government cleanup was ordered. The company that owned the mine eventually went bankrupt.

Truth – part 2

You may have heard the story of the blind men and the elephant. In case you have not heard it, here is my abbreviated version:

The elephant came to town one day and the blind men, not knowing what an elephant was, went over to check it out. The person who held the elephant's tail declared that the elephant is like a rope. The one that touched the leg said, "No! The elephant is like a pillar." The one that touched the ear said, "Both of you don't know what you are talking about, because the elephant is just like a giant hand fan." The one that touched the tusk declared that the elephant was like a solid pipe. They began to argue among themselves, each declaring only he knew the whole truth and the others were clueless.

A few thoughts came to my mind when I first read this story:

One, if we are ever fortunate enough to grasp the truth, we should be aware that at best, we are only scratching the surface of the entire truth. It is impossible to grasp the whole absolute truth in our limited human mind. What we know is finite. What we do not know is infinite.

Two, it is possible that diametrically opposed views on a subject could both be right. Some time ago, one group of scientists were declaring that light is a wave. Another group of scientists said that light is a particle. Today, we know that light can be both a wave and a particle.

If we begin with the above two points in mind, then we would approach any matter with the understanding that each of us may hold only a piece of the puzzle. When we each bring our piece of the puzzle and collaborate, then at least we have some chance of getting closer to the bigger picture. But if we hold on religiously to our small piece of the puzzle, and naively and arrogantly think that the small piece we embrace is the whole truth and the only truth, we are depriving ourselves and others of seeing the bigger picture.

Truth – part 3

You are assigned to pick up a philosopher from the airport, but you have no clue what the philosopher looks like. How will you know whom to pick up from the multitude of people out there? Even if you were to come face to face with the philosopher, how would you know that was the philosopher? Likewise, if one day you discovered the complete truth, how would you know it was the complete truth? We are limited to our three dimensions in space and one dimension in time. Can we still grasp the whole truth, even with these limitations?

Plato's *Allegory of the Cave* is useful in demonstrating that knowledge gained through the senses is no more than opinion, and that, in order to have real knowledge, we must gain it through philosophical reasoning.

Mind your own business

There are two kinds of business in the world: my business and other's business. Unhappiness always occurs when I stray from my business. I have no right being in other's business because I don't have the complete picture. Therefore, I try to concern myself with what is my business and only in aspects that I can do something about. Things that are not within my control are not my business, hence not my concern. It is not my business either to live up to what other people think I ought to accomplish. What people say about me are their perception and their business.

"What is too sublime for you, do not seek;

do not reach into things that are hidden from you.

What is committed to you, pay heed to;

what is hidden is not your concern.

In matters that are beyond you do not meddle,

when you have been shown more than you can understand." (Sirach 3:21 - 23)

Cocktail parties

Cocktail parties are like dogs' sniff tests. Dogs sniff each other's butts to get detailed information about the other dog. The aroma emitted from a dog's butt reveals the dog's vital information such as health status and temperament. Likewise, people in cocktail parties go around "sniffing each other's butts" to ascertain each other's worth.

True colors

Warren Buffet once said, "Only when the tide goes out do you discover who's been swimming naked." Our true self is only revealed when we lose whatever that has been shielding us - be it our sense of identity from our job titles or our sense of security from our financial assets. Adversity has a knack for getting us better acquainted with ourselves.

Is there any situation you see yourself being abusive?

In August 1971, undergraduate volunteers were randomly assigned to play the role of either prisoner or guard in a mock prison. It did not take long for those playing the role of guards to become abusive. Even though the experiment was planned for 14 days; it had to be canceled after 6 days due to what was happening to the volunteers. The simulated prison environment brought out the worst in the participants. The guards, for example, began humiliating and psychologically abusing the prisoners. This is despite the fact volunteers were chosen specifically based on their moderate demeanor, lack of prior trouble, and representative status to their peers. Years later, Professor Philip Zimbardo, who conducted this infamous Stanford Prison Study, said, "It wasn't until much later that I realized how far into my prison role I was at that point -- that I was thinking like a prison superintendent rather than a research psychologist." According to Zimbardo, most people do not see themselves as evil, but could be compelled to do evil in a situation.

In 1959, John Howard Griffin changed the color of his skin temporarily to become a black man. He traveled through the harshly segregated southern states of America to see what life was really like for blacks. He did not change his name or identity. Nothing changed except the color of his skin. After only a few weeks as a black man, he felt depression and hopelessness, due to racial prejudice and discrimination. Six weeks into the experiment, Griffin decided to end the project and return home. Just temporarily 'losing his white color' was sufficient to emotionally drain him in a matter of weeks. It is hard to be immune to how one is treated.

Life

Forrest Gump's mom said, "Life is like a box of chocolates; you never know what you are going to get." I say, "Life is like a stock market; you know what you are going to get." Life has its ups (bull market), life has its downs (bear market), but for the most part, life is more or less the same (sideways market).

A cynic may define life as a sexually transmitted terminal disease. Is the cynic wrong?

Power of the crowd

Geese in formation can fly 75 percent farther than they can alone. There is strength in numbers.

The Asch conformity experiments demonstrated the power of conformity in groups. People conform either because they want to fit in with the group or because self-doubt leads them to believe the majority has to be right. Human see, human do. Conventions are created by the convictions of the majority. Like it or not, the majority defines what is *normal* and the majority can be 'right', even when they are wrong.

Investor and philanthropist George Soros realized that despite being wrong, investors could still influence reality to the point where they could even become right. He called this phenomenon "reflexivity." The participants' views influence the course of events, and the course of events influences the participants' views. The influence is continuous and circular; that is what turns it into a feedback loop. And that means the success of an idea will be determined more by what people believe than by what clear facts dictate... or what previous outcomes would suggest.

"Normal is getting dressed in clothes that you buy for work, driving through traffic in a car that you are still paying for, in order to get to a job that you need so you can pay for the clothes, car and the house that you leave empty all day in order to afford to live in it." (Ellen Goodman)

Acting against your own interest

There is a breed of wasp that lays their eggs in the abdomen of arachnids. Once inseminated, the spiders are thought to be influenced by the release of a mind-altering hormone that makes them protect the wasp eggs at any cost, even though they face imminent death once these eggs hatch.

The microbe *toxoplasma gondii* can sexually reproduce only in the cat gut, and for it to get there; the pathogen's rodent host must be eaten. As such, within three weeks of infection with that microbe, the rodent loses all fear of cat odor, and is instead drawn to the smell of cat urine.

There are other examples where an organism hijacks their host's brain to make them act in ways that benefit the organism, but at the expense of the host. Can humans be victims of such organisms too?

The illusion of free will

Benjamin Libet, a researcher in the physiology department of the University of California, San Francisco, wired up subjects to measure their brain activities via electrodes on their scalp and asked them to choose to perform a simple hand movement when they felt like it. The subjects recorded the time at which they made a conscious decision to move their hand. Libet found evidence of brain activity initiating the movement hundreds of milliseconds before a conscious decision was reported. His experiments seem to show that a conscious decision didn't cause the movement, because our brains seem to initiate an action before we are even aware of wanting to make it.

Do you really have a choice if it is influenced by what other people think? Have you never been manipulated into buying things you don’t really need? Are you really making the decision, or are your peers or even your kids making the decision for you? Cambridge Analytica bragged that it had up to 5000 data points on every U.S. voter, with which they claimed they could influence voter behavior. How many of the key decisions in your life were already made for you by your parents or the government? According to Philip B. Heymann of Harvard Law School, "We live in a world in which relatively few people—maybe 500 or 1,000—make the important decisions."

We did not choose our genes, and we cannot deny the profound effect they have on us. The Minnesota Study of Twins Reared Apart found that identical twins that are reared apart had the same chance of being similar as twins who were raised together. This supports the argument that genetic factors and inheritance play a large role in the development of individuals and the interests and characteristics they show.

We did not choose if, when and where we were going to be born. We do not choose when, where, and how we die.* And yet, we believe we have choice for all the stuff in between, despite the influence that genes, sibling order, gender, race, and nationality have on us?

*The exception here is when a person decides to commit suicide and succeeds.

"Everything is determined, the beginning as well as the end, by forces over which we have no control. It is determined for insects as well as for the stars. Human beings, vegetables or cosmic dust, we all dance to a mysterious tune, intoned in the distance by an invisible piper." (Albert Einstein)

Pride

Sometimes we may ponder about something for days, and then, out of the blue, we get an insight. Our pride leads us to think that we are the source of the insight. If we were humble, we would accept that we were mere recipients of it.

Being single

"The need to find another human being to share one's life with has always puzzled me. Maybe because I'm so interesting all by myself. With that being said, may you find as much happiness with each other as I find on my own." (Sheldon, The Big Bang Theory)

It is not easy being single. That's why some people cave in and get married. But they discover later that marriage does not solve whatever issues they had before, and eventually, the marriage falls apart. Some end in divorce and others in separation. And just because a couple remains married does not necessarily mean it is a happy marriage. The happy and successful marriages are those where the singles were already good by themselves, but found another single, where the fusion magnified their already good lives.

A cynic will say that the primary cause for divorce is marriage. Is the cynic wrong?

Void, empty, and unbusy

When I asked my friend why he is so motivated to get hitched, he mentioned that there is a void that needs to be filled. When people visit me, many suggest that I should get furniture to fill the empty space in my living room. When I greet people and ask what is going on; many frequently reply: “Keeping busy.” People seem to take pride in keeping themselves busy.

Does a void need to be filled? Why do people feel uncomfortable with emptiness? Music is sound interspersed with silence. If it is incessant sound, it becomes noise. Likewise in life, periods of activities need to be accompanied by periods of stillness. In building muscles, the rest or recovery period is just as important as pumping iron.

Why do we think we need to be perpetually busy? If time is money, aren’t we broke if we are always busy and have no time? Recall the story of the lumberjack who was attempting to saw a tree? When the bystander pointed out that he could be more efficient if he just sharpened the saw, Mr. Lumberjack replied, "I am too busy sawing to take time to sharpen my saw."

“Those who are wise won’t be busy, and those who are too busy can’t be wise.” (Lin Yutang)

La dolce far niente

La dolce far niente is the Italian concept of the sweetness of doing nothing. Italians are not the only ones who are proficient in the art of loafing. It is an art, though, and usually not mastered by individuals that chase after fame or fortune. Specialists in the art of loafing know that the enjoyment of *la dolce far niente* costs less than the enjoyment of luxury. The enjoyment of loafing does not cost money. The best things in life are free. So is loafing.

Do something!

Saddam Hussein wakes up one morning bored and says: We gotta ***do something!*** He invades Kuwait. American troops kick his arse back to where it belongs, but Osama Bin Laden finds the presence of Americans in the region as desecrating his holy land. So he says: We gotta ***do something!*** The Twin Towers come down. Now, it is our commander-in-chief's turn to say: We gotta

do something! He eventually attacks Iraq. Back home, our economy is in the toilet, so the Federal Chairman says: We gotta ***do something!*** He brings down the interest rates. With the easy finance, Mrs. Doe sees all her neighbors making easy money flipping properties. She looks at John, her loser husband, and says: We gotta ***do something!*** John Doe goes to the bank and says he wants to flip, not burgers, but houses. The banker asks:

Do you have any source of income? *No.*

Do you have a job? *No.*

Do you have any assets? *No.*

All right! Just sign here and the house is yours!

John Doe goes home, head held up high, and tells his wife: "You see, I am not a loser. I can ***do something!***"

From the president to the terrorist, from the Federal Chairman to John Doe, wouldn't we all be better off if they did not ***do something***? The next time someone tells you

"We gotta ***do something***!" Please resist the temptation to ***do something!***

Seasons come and go without us having to do anything. Flowers bloom and trees bear fruits without us having to do anything. An embryo develops following its own rhythm. Yet, humans have the illusion that doing something is *always* better than doing nothing. This is known as action bias. The Chernobyl nuclear plant explosion began with an experiment to increase reactor safety. The easiest and best way to benefit from the nutrition of a fruit is to just eat it. But action-biased humans will juice it or engage in activities to rob the fruit of its fiber, nutrition, or both before consuming it. The Great Pacific Garbage Patch is about 1.6 million square kilometers in size. That is two times the size of Texas or three times the size of France. This humongous garbage did not just magically appear. It was the result of humans working hard. Human-made debris is not only in the oceans and on earth, but on space as well. The earth is beautiful. Sit back, give thanks, and enjoy the beauty instead of working hard to pollute it.

Less, not more

When you are relaxed, you need to breathe less, not more.

When you are physically fit, your heart needs to work less, not more.

When you are healthy in mind, body, and spirit, you need less of everything, not more.

About bees

A worker bee born during the summer period only survives about 6 weeks before it dies of exhaustion. Remember karōshi? A queen bee, on the other hand, can live up to five years. A worker bee and a queen bee are genetically identical, but differ in which genes are activated. Honey bees genetically alter their bodies via nutrition. A few of the larvae are chosen and provided royal jelly, which is nutritiously superior to what the others get. The ones fed with the royal food have the potential to become a queen. The drones or male bees serve only to mate with the queen; after that they die or are expelled. The queen bee serves to lay eggs; the majority of which will become worker bees with the sole purpose of serving the colony.

Work

"Oh, you hate your job? Why didn't you say so? There's a support group for that. It's called everybody, and they meet at the bar." (Drew Carey)

The major medical causes of karōshi deaths are heart attack and stroke due to stress. A study by researchers at the Harvard Business School and Stanford's Graduate School of Business revealed that anxiety about employment may contribute to over 120,000 deaths each year. This is more than death via diabetes, Alzheimer's, or the flu.

In the book *In Search of Excellence*, the authors report that most people desperately need meaning in their lives, and will sacrifice a great deal to institutions that will provide it to them. They also went on to say that the infrastructure of most American companies is almost consistently unable to provide meaning or any sense of worth to its employees.

Steve Jobs on work:

"Your work is going to fill a large part of your life, and the only way to be truly satisfied is to do what you believe is great work. And the only way to do great work is to love what you do."

"If you haven't found it yet, keep looking. Don't settle."

"Think of the greatest thing you can imagine. Do that."

Who is the slave here?

Diogenes is my favorite philosopher. One day, his slave, Manes, ran away. People advised Diogenes that he should go after Manes. But Diogenes, being a cynic, rationalized differently. If the slave ran away, he must have figured out that he must be able to do better without the master. If the slave can do better without the master, shouldn't the master be able to do better without the slave? If not, who is the real slave here?

"It would be a very absurd thing for Manes to be able to live without Diogenes, but for Diogenes not to be able to live without Manes." (Diogenes)

Runaway slave

"I think the person who takes a job in order to live - that is to say, for the money - has turned himself into a slave." (Joseph Campbell)

In the old days, you had the master and the slave.

Today, you have the employer and the employee.

In the old days, the master provided food and lodging in return for the work provided by the slave.

Today, the employer provides a salary in return for the work provided by the employee.

In the old days, you had the house slaves and field slaves.

Today, you have the white-collar employees and blue-collar employees.

In the old days, some slaves tried to escape.

The few that succeeded must have shouted jubilantly: "Free at last! Free at last! Free at last!"

Today, some employees try to escape the grind.

The few that succeed probably also shout ecstatically: "Free at last! Free at last! Free at last!"

I know someone who did.

"It is difficult to free fools from the chains they revere." (Voltaire)

Dust in the wind

The kakapo is a kind of parrot in New Zealand that has forgotten that it has forgotten to fly. Why? Because there were no predators and food was easy, hence no reason to fly. Over generations, the skill gets lost. Just like how the Kakapo has forgotten that it has forgotten how to fly; ever wondered if we humans have forgotten what we have forgotten - some of the capabilities that our ancestors may have possessed?

Thousands of years before Europeans even began ocean exploration, the Polynesians had successfully figured out a way to navigate the ocean without the use of compasses or modern technology. They had to memorize the motion of specific stars, weather, times of travel, wildlife species (which would congregate at particular positions), directions of swells on the ocean, colors of the sea and sky, how clouds would cluster at some locations of islands and angles for approaching harbors. Are there any humans today with these skills?

The Romans mastered the skill of building aqueducts and built several across their empire. But during the Dark Ages, many of these aqueducts were destroyed and their stones re-used for new buildings. The main reason the aqueducts were destroyed was that no one knew how to use them. They were deemed much more valuable as building material. Even the Roman system of urban sanitation and techniques of road construction was forgotten.

Knowledge is just as fragile as an empire or a life.

Rise of the machines

Many people are willing to give up their privacy, time, and money to utilize technology. As devices get smarter, humans will not, at least in those areas where the devices are getting smarter. Eventually, the domain of expertise where robots can make quicker and better decisions than humans will expand to the point that humans will not be needed in most activities. As the mathematician, Claude Shannon said: “I visualize a time when we will be to robots what dogs are to humans, and I’m rooting for the machines.”

But dogs serve a purpose to humans. I don’t see humans serving any purpose to robots. Do you?

Wasted resources

On July 20th, 1969, Apollo 11 became the first spacecraft to meet the goal of sending humans to land on the moon and returning them safely to Earth. Today, our cell phones have more computing power than the computers used during the Apollo era. What are we doing with all that power? Finding rare Pokémon? Poking friends on Facebook? Following on Twitter people that don’t know you or you don’t even like? Viewing mindless videos on YouTube or posting on Instagram?

The importance of…

Only a person who has lost the Olympic gold medal by seven-hundredths of a second will appreciate the importance of milliseconds. Only someone who has missed a flight by a few minutes recognizes the importance of every minute. Timing matters. A right decision made a second later can be fatal.

Unseen, unknown

Just because humans cannot see infrared color, doesn't mean it does not exist. Just because we cannot hear any sound below 20 hertz or above 20,000 hertz, does not mean they do not exist. Hence to declare that something does not exist because we are unable to sense or fathom it is hubris, dumb, or both. Science can only prove something does exist. So, to be adamant something does not exist is unscientific.

About 8 million blood cells die in your body every second, and the same number are born each second. We don't have anything to do with it consciously. You may decide what to eat. However, once you have eaten, do you have any control over how the body breaks down the food, digests it, and is finally absorbed? Though we may have control over some of the human body's functioning; much of the essential functions are beyond our mind and will. More is unknown than known.

Even experts make mistakes – part one

In Thomas Kuhn's book *The Structure of Scientific Revolution*, he wrote that experts resist new paradigms for approximately 30 years – a whole generation. He found that the worst offenders were the experts within an industry who would resist anything that differed from their accepted dogma.

There was a time when the science in place was based on the concept that the atom was the smallest particle in the universe. Later, it was discovered that the atom itself contained smaller particles.

Before the BSE (commonly known as mad cow disease) outbreak in the UK, most scientists thought it was safe for the rendered remains of animal carcasses to be fed to herbivores.

Does proficiency in mathematics and science alone help us in making better decisions every time? Long-Term Capital Management (LTCM) was a hedge fund company founded by two math wizards who won the Nobel Prize in economics. They came up with a "black box" based on quantitative mathematics. According to their math, the chance of them going bust was 1 in 10 to the power of 24. And yet, they did go bust.

When the Monty Hall problem appeared in the Parade magazine, approximately 10,000 readers, including nearly 1,000 with PhDs, wrote to the magazine claiming the published solution was wrong.

Katja Schneider, the director of the State Art Museum of Moritzburg in Saxony-Anhalt, was confident that a painting was the work of a master artist, Ernst Wilhelm Nay, who was famous for using blotches of color. It turned out to be the work of Banghi, a chimp.

Even experts make mistakes - part two

In late 2008, during a briefing by academics at the London School of Economics on the turmoil on the international markets, the Queen asked, "If these things were so large, how come everyone missed it?" Professor Luis Garicano, director of research at the London School of Economics' management department, told the Queen, "At every stage, someone was relying on somebody else and everyone thought they were doing the right thing."

This seems to be the recurring theme: One so-called expert comes up with something that other experts begin to use as a reference, without double-checking, and very soon, it becomes assumed to be the truth, fact or benchmark.

When physicist Richard Feynman was working on a new theory of beta decay, he noticed something surprising. For years, experts had been saying that beta decay occurred in a particular way, but when Feynman actually ran the experiments, he kept getting a different result. Eventually, Feynman investigated the original data that all of the experts were basing their theory on and discovered that the study was flawed. For years, nobody had bothered to read or repeat the original study! All of the experts just kept quoting one another and used their mutual opinions as justification for the theory. Then Feynman came along and turned everything upside down, simply because he did the calculations himself.

Even experts make mistake – part three

Theranos, a blood-testing startup, had the following distinguished men on its board of directors: Henry Kissinger, James Mattis, and George Shultz.

Theranos had also secured the investments of Walmart's Walton family, the media mogul Rupert Murdoch, the Cox family -- who own the media conglomerate Cox Enterprises -- and Larry Ellison, the founder of Oracle.

On September 9th, 2013, Theranos and Walgreens announced a long-term partnership to bring access to Theranos' new lab testing service through Walgreens pharmacies nationwide.

It would be easy to feel safe in the company of the experts and to invest in Theranos, if one had the opportunity. It would also be conceivable to pay for the Theranos blood testing service and to believe the results of the tests. Unfortunately, we cannot rely on experts, or anyone else for that matter, to make any crucial decisions.

On June 15th, 2018, Theranos founder, Elizabeth Holmes and her former Chief Operating Officer, Ramesh Balwani, were charged with two counts of conspiracy to commit wire fraud and nine counts of wire fraud. According to the indictment, the charges stem from allegations that Holmes and her former Chief Operating Officer engaged in a multi-million dollar scheme to defraud investors, and a separate scheme to defraud doctors and patients.

Experts and leaders are humans and as such capable of making mistakes, just like all of us.

Simple solutions

Robert Harrison, of Highburton, West Yorkshire, took pictures of the Earth that impressed NASA. They thought Mr. Harrison must have used a homemade rocket to take such spectacular shots from over 20 miles above the Earth's surface. In reality, it was a simple solution consisting primarily of a digital camera, duct tape, a helium balloon, and a GPS tracking device. His total cost was about 500 pounds.

The annual Advanced Technology Education Remotely Operated Vehicle Competition, an event sponsored by NASA and the Navy, was established to encourage and identify the country's top engineering talent. In 2004, the winners of the competition were a team from an unknown high school in Arizona. That team was made up of four teenagers and three of the four were undocumented immigrants. They did not win against other high school teams though. They, in fact, chose to compete at the college-level and beat the MIT team (consisting of 12 students). The cost of their robot was about $800. The MIT team, sponsored by ExxonMobil, made a robot which cost at least $11,000. Unfunded, undocumented and "uneducated" compared to the other college-level teams – the high school students still won. How is it possible? Thinking outside the box! Formal education can sometimes lead students to think within certain parameters. How do you think university-level engineering students would have solved the water leak issue of the robot? The four kids from Hayden High

School resorted to tampons to soak up the water.

If a person develops diabetes due to diet and lifestyle choices, modern medicine's solution is to prescribe the person drugs. The simplest solution will have been to remove what caused the disease in the first place.

"All other things being equal, the simplest solution tends to be the best one." (Occam's "Razor")

Treating others

Do not treat others how you like to be treated, but rather, treat others how they want to be treated. A masochist is not going to appreciate a normal partner or another masochist partner. Pair a masochist with a sadist. Then, you will have two satisfied people.

Heroes and villains

People destined for a different path from the mainstream usually suffered rejection, persecution, and even death. Heroes and villains may suffer the same fate. For example, Jesus Christ was crucified with two thieves. In 1431, Joan of Arc was declared a heretic and burned at the stake. In 1920, three miracles attributed to Joan were finally authenticated and she was formally declared a saint. Once seen as a heretic, now as a martyr. Who are the heroes today that will be declared as villains tomorrow, and who are the villains today that will be declared as heroes tomorrow?

Distinctions reminder

Correlation does not imply causation. Absence of evidence is not evidence of absence. Legal does not mean moral. Alone does not mean lonely. Content does not mean lazy. Unity does not mean uniformity. Random does not mean chaotic. Simple does not mean easy. Difficult does not mean impossible. Inevitable does not mean imminent. Confident does not mean correct.

Expensive does not mean good nor does free mean bad. Humility is not cowardice. Meekness is not weakness. Precision is useless if you are not accurate. Efficiency is useless if you are not effective. Speed is detrimental if you are going in the wrong direction. One can be spontaneous without being reckless. One can be fit, but not healthy. Favor health span over life span. Focus on probability not possibility, knowing that probability is not certainty. It's not having what you want. It's wanting what you have. When you lose, don't lose the lesson. Success is never final, failure is never fatal. But failure to change might be. Don't let what you cannot do interfere with what you can do. Favor character over achievement, and function before fashion. Be more concerned with your character than your reputation, because your character is what you really are, while your reputation is merely what others think you are. Be able to separate facts from opinion, signal from noise and wheat from chaff. Some people erroneously conclude something is meaningless when it is actually, an enigma. Some people grow old without growing up.

Some people can be sincere and sincerely wrong. Some people can be looking without seeing, talking without speaking, hearing without listening, and reading without understanding. Don't mistake mood for reality or mistake perception as permanent truth. Don't mistake busyness for productivity or the trappings of success for success itself. Don't mistake the right to be heard as including the right to be taken seriously. Just because you can, does not mean you should. Pyrrhic victory is not victory.

Improved versions

<u>Karma is a bitch.</u>

People erroneously think that karma only applies to misdeeds. If we think, say, and do good, we will reap benefits.

Improved version: Karma is like a boomerang.

<u>Everything in moderation.</u>

Do you take poison in moderation or murder in moderation?

Improved version: Everything after consideration.

<u>You learn to walk by falling.</u>

Do pilots learn to fly by crashing planes? Just because we fall while learning to walk, does not mean that we actually learn to walk by falling. If that was true, you will still be falling when you walk. Maybe you do…

Improved version: You learn to walk by not falling.

<u>Ignorance is bliss.</u>

The legal principle of *ignorantia legis neminem excusat* (ignorance of law excuses no one) is derived from Roman law. So a person is still liable even if they claimed ignorance of the law they broke. I am sure there are things that have happened in your life that made you say, "I wish I'd known then what I know now." The art of living, therefore, consists in acquiring wisdom in areas that we are responsible for and where we can make a difference, and choosing to be ignorant of the rest.

Improved version: Selective ignorance is bliss.

Money is the root of all evil.

Is there anything wrong in wanting money so that you could feed the hungry or shelter the homeless? Evil exists because we are ignorant, and hence unaware of the full ramifications of our actions or inactions.

Improved version: Ignorance is the root of evil.

Biases

Recall question 5 in the beginning of the book? Did you entertain the possibility that the nurse is a male nurse and is the girl's dad?* Most people have difficulty figuring out the answer, and psychologists attribute it to gender bias. A few other biases, out of the litany of biases out there, are: action bias, anchoring bias, confirmation bias, hindsight bias, and self-serving bias.

The fact that you bought this book and are reading it implies you may not be influenced by the bandwagon effect. Kudos to you!

*Another possible answer to question 5 could be that the nurse is a female and the girl has lesbian parents.

Precious present

Future is the summation of all the present. Irrespective of apparent short-term wins and losses, eventually our lives gravitate toward the sum of our choices. Therefore, if you want your future to be happy, you have to be happy today and every day. Do not put it off until you retire, or when you strike the lottery, or when you meet that special someone, or till someday. Someday may be too late. Make the someday, today! Do not keep anything for a special occasion because every day is a special occasion. It is better to live rich than to die rich. Only in the present can you take action. So do not put off until tomorrow what needs to be done today.

"If you are depressed, you are living in the past. If you are anxious, you are living in the future. If you are at peace, you are living in the present." (Lao Tzu)

Memorial services

I understand that memorial services serve as a closure to the family members and friends of the deceased. Despite that, I find memorial services meaningless. If I am worth the time for you to dress up, commute to and from the memorial service, and spend the time at the memorial service, I would rather you spend it with me, while I am alive. If I am not good to look at while I am alive, I am certainly not going to be good to look at in the casket. Glowing comments about a person in the form of an obituary is not as helpful to the person as immediate feedback when the person is still alive. You never know: An honest heartfelt appreciation or kindness shown to a person at the right time might have prevented the person's early demise.

End of life – part one

Bronnie Ware worked in palliative care in Australia for several years, tending to the needs of those who were dying, being with them for the last three to twelve weeks of their lives. When questioned about any regrets they had, or anything they would do differently, common themes surfaced again and again. Here are the most common five:

1. I wish I'd had the courage to live a life true to myself, not the life others expected of me.

2. I wish I hadn't worked so hard.

3. I wish I'd had the courage to express my feelings.

4. I wish I had stayed in touch with my friends.

5. I wish that I had let myself be happier.

According to Bronnie, most people had not honored even a half of their dreams, and had to die knowing that it was due to choices they had made, or not made. Every male patient that she nursed wished they hadn't worked so hard. They missed out on their children's youth and their partner's companionship. Many people suppressed their feelings in order to keep peace with others. As a result, they settled for a mediocre existence and never became who they were truly capable of becoming. There were many deep regrets about not giving friendships thc time and effort that they deserved. Everyone misses their friends when they are dying.

Bronnie's patients knew they were dying. Whether you realize it or not, we are all dying. We just don't know when we will take our last breath. This should not lead us to despondency, but rather nudge us to make every day of our life count.

End of life – part two

They say that our entire life flashes before us, just before we die.

If you deliberately choose to play your entire life slowly now, while you are still alive, is there anything you feel sorry for? If so, wouldn't it be prudent to seek reconciliation now?

The moment one is diagnosed with a terminal illness and has a limited number of days to live, the priorities change.

Our life is a challenge and a project. The challenge is to figure out our mission in life, or who we really are. The project is to fulfill that mission, or to be our authentic self. If we remain committed to the process of being our true self, then before the end of our lives, we may become the distilled, crystallized versions of who we really are.

"Let us so live that when we come to die even the undertaker will be sorry." (Mark Twain)

End of life – part three

From Mona Simpson's eulogy for Steve Jobs: "Before embarking, he'd looked at his sister Patty, then for a long time at his children, then at his life's partner, Laurene, and then over their shoulders past them. Steve's final words were:

"OH WOW. OH WOW. OH WOW.""

From the book *Edison: Inventing the Century* by Neil Baldwin: "Towards the end, he emerged from a coma, opened his eyes, looked upwards and said to Mina, "It is very beautiful over there.""

The monkey and a flower

There is a proverb in the Malay language that advises one not to give a flower to a monkey. The monkey doesn't appreciate it. Whenever, I fail to appreciate a book I am reading, a movie I am watching, or a chance encounter, I ask myself, could I be the monkey?

Pass it on

'When someone shares with you something of value, you have an obligation to share it with others." (Unknown)

You may have the wisdom to know what the right thing to do is. You may also have the fortitude to execute your wise decision. However, despite your right decisions and corresponding actions, you are not immune to the bad decisions and actions or inactions of others. No person is an island. Our destinies are intertwined. In my book, *The Happy Minimalist*, I said the following:

"There are at least two reasons we suffer: because of our own mistakes and because of the mistakes of others. If I drive under the influence of alcohol, and consequently crash and am paralyzed for life, that was my mistake. If someone else was drunk and rear-ended me, consequently incapacitating me, that is what I call suffering because of the mistake of others. As you can see, it is not sufficient that we alone are educated, enlightened, and disciplined. It is in our own best interest to ensure others are, as well.

There are countless examples of how the action or inaction of even a few can have grave impact on the rest. The financial meltdown of 2007 is a good example of that. If we want to realize the full benefits of our right actions, it is imperative that we attempt to enlighten others as well."

Monica England's research on crossword puzzles pointed to the existence of a collective consciousness. As crossword puzzles are completed by a critical mass of people, that information becomes a part of the collective consciousness and can be transmitted from one mind to another. Hence, with the passage of time, as more people complete the puzzles, it becomes more easily solved by others.

Law of Diffusion of Innovation suggests 15 to18 percent market penetration seems to be the tipping point. Sharing your knowledge or the good works of others, with as many people you know is a way to reach the critical mass or tipping point sooner. So pass it on.

Lessons from friends and strangers

Note: Names of my friends are not the actual names. What they shared with me are unedited except for the name.

What do we really need?

Years ago, when I caught up with a friend over lunch, he disclosed to me that he had recently undergone an operation where they removed his bile duct. Apparently, you do not need it! I know it has been said that you do not need the appendix, too. You can survive without hair, without hands or legs. You can even survive with just one kidney. Helen Keller demonstrated that despite being deaf and blind, one could lead an inspiring life.

Getting your priorities right

Once I was in Grenoble, France on a business trip. Jenny, my counterpart at the European marketing centre came to me and said that she had some work to complete before we leave for dinner and that we should plan to leave at about 7 p.m. Minutes before 7 p.m., she shuts off her computer and comes over and says, “Peter, let’s leave.” “Were you able to complete what you were supposed to complete?” I asked. She said “No,” and then said, “You are only going to be here for a few days. Work will always be here. So, let’s go.”

That left a lasting impression on me – on getting one’s priorities right. Months later, someone that I knew from Australia was visiting. The last night she was here she had no plans, so I offered to take her out. Carly (not the real name), my boss’s boss, was expecting something from me before I left for the day. I knew I could not complete it in time to meet up with my friend that was visiting. Though Carly can be quite demanding, and some were quite afraid of approaching her, I went to her and informed her that I wouldn’t be able to complete that day what she needed, as I had an appointment, and left the office to take my friend out.

“Things that matter most must never be at the mercy of things that matter least.”

(Goethe)

Knowing your value

A former female colleague of mine sent me an e-mail after surviving a retrenchment exercise in her department. Part of it follows:

"I can kinda see how divorced women feel. The ones that kinda have their lives built around their husbands. When they get divorced, they feel worthless, unattractive, etc. But they still look the same and have the same good qualities. I had to really sit down and teach myself that my talents/capabilities are mine, with or without the job."

Perspective

From an e-mail from a friend of mine whose wife had passed on:

"To my neighbors, my friends:

Please accept my thanks for the compassionate support you have all given me. What may seem to you to have been a sudden death was, in reality, a longer story. Jenny did not lose her battle with cancer; she actually won. Why? Because seven years ago her oncologist told Jenny she could expect to live two months to two years max. So it wasn't a battle; it was a dance, a dance that lasted much longer than prognosticated. And the music was good."

Déjà vu

Many years ago, I received the following from my friend, who is a geneticist:

"Sad. A friend of mine passed away while diving in Malaysia.

Today I attended a tea session by our chairman who spoke about our future career possibilities, I was still contemplating it, but now I think maybe there is no need to contemplate much since life is so unpredictable... and the same can be said for research: unpredictable. Really no need think too far ahead in future."

Then, the very next day, he sent me this message:

“I sometimes experience déjà vu. It is as though life is a pre-written script, designed to be invisible to us in general. But during "lapses", we catch a glimpse of the future and when that scene of the future finally arrives, we get the déjà vu. With this interpretation, then we just need to walk down the path that is natural to each of us, and no need worry about the destination which is fixed anyway”.

Spontaneous remission

After solving my plumbing issue, my plumber chatted with me for a while, during which he shared with me that once he missed his doctor’s appointment to remove a mole on his chest. His doctor had advised him to remove the mole because it could be, or was, cancerous. In any case, he delayed making another appointment to get the mole removed until, one day, he noticed that it was gone. I am not sure if that can be classified as spontaneous remission, but spontaneous remissions do happen. My suspicion is that it actually may be happening more often than we realize. None of us examine or test ourselves on a daily basis, so how would we know if we have cancer or some disease today that disappeared before our next medical check-up?

In the book *Mind Over Medicine*, Dr. Lissa Rankin M.D. provides scientific proof that one can heal oneself. Dr. Rankin recognized the body's innate ability to self-repair and how we can facilitate the self-repair with the power of the mind. In clinical trials, 18 to 80 percent of patients can get better due to the placebo effect. And this effect is not restricted to just fake pills but fake surgery as well. The power of belief works both ways. The opposite of placebo effect is nocebo effect; hence be mindful of what beliefs you choose to entertain and dwell upon, because they can affect your body's physiology.

Listen

A physiotherapist friend of mine mentioned something interesting that caught my attention:

"The body will continue to compensate, and can function with about 95 percent dysfunction. It is only in that last 5 percent that the body cracks the shits and presents as pain (in most cases)."

"How can I ensure I don't wait till I reach that breaking point?" I asked.

"Learn to listen to your body," she advised.

Black hole or bright moon

Part of a homily by Fr. Christopher Soh from the Church of St. Ignatius Church in Singapore:

"...my simple mind finds it helpful to compare a black hole with the moon. Which often appears to us as a brightly shining object. High up in the sky. This is even though, as we all know, the moon doesn't actually produce any light on its own. It shines only by reflecting the rays of the sun. And the moon is able to do this because its own gravitational pull is weak. Weak enough to allow the light falling upon it to escape. So that others can see it.

In sharp contrast to the brightly shining moon, however, a black hole is always shrouded in darkness. It does not shine. This is because its gravity is so strong that any light falling upon it is instantly absorbed by it. Sucked into the black hole itself. Unable to escape. As a result, the black hole remains invisible. We know it's there only by observing its effects on the objects around it.

The moon, because of its weakness, is able to reflect the sun's light. But a black hole is simply too strong to shine."

Lessons from traveling

Pay to learn

"We pay the price for the lessons we learn." That's what Ahab, a hotel staffer from the Magi Hotel in Cairo, Egypt, told me in response for not refunding the full amount for a trip that I canceled.

Universal

There are some things that I found everywhere, irrespective of whether it is a developed economy or an emerging economy:

- Beggars and homeless people.

- People addicted to their cell phones such that they do not pay attention to their customers, the people they are with, or even the road.

- Bad diet. Most people eat badly, meaning food laden with sugar, salt, and bad fat. Fast food and processed food is pervasive too. Consequently, the same three diseases plague most countries: Diabetes, high blood pressure, and heart disease. During a carnival in Panama, a guy threw a piece of hot dog to a stray dog; the dog sniffed it and wouldn't eat it. But people were devouring these hot dogs with much gusto. Humans gobbling what dogs fear to eat. The International Agency for Research on Cancer (IARC) has classified processed meat as a carcinogen. Processed meat includes hot dogs, ham, bacon, sausage, and some deli meats. I guess the stray dog already knew that.

- Climate change. People all over the world acknowledged that the temperatures have gotten higher, especially in the last five years.

On the positive side, people are welcoming, kind, and definitely not as bad as you may have been led to believe by the media.

Regulations

People who are against all government regulations probably have never lived in developing countries. When you don't have emission standards, you can have black fumes out of buses like in Guatemala. Even with regulations, incidents like what happened to the water in Flint, Michigan, can happen. Can you imagine the water quality without any regulations? Why do you think a 7.0 magnitude earthquake has a more devastating effect in developing countries compared to developed countries? Proper building codes, as well as adherence to the code, mitigates risks.

Tips

There are usually more places of accommodation than what Google maps show you.

Don't assume that hotels are more expensive than hostels. I have found hotels that are cheaper than hostels. The disadvantage of a hotel is that it is very unlikely you will be able to use the kitchen.

When you stay long, that is a month or more, in a place, it gives you some latitude to negotiate with the accommodation owner. The cheapest place I stayed after negotiation was $3 million VND a month at a hotel in

Sapa, Vietnam in 2018. That worked out to $4.32 USD per day.

Don't assume that streetside eating is cheaper than at a restaurant. Street vendors may charge you more, knowing that you are a tourist. For example, I have asked for the price of sticky rice at many street vendors, and all except one quoted me more than $10,000 VND. I was able to get sticky rice at a restaurant for $10,000 VND. A local told me he could buy it for $5,000 VND though it was different and didn't taste that good. As of this writing, $10,000 VND is about 0.43 USD.

When it comes to groceries, try to find a supermarket and purchase food there, as usually it will be cleaner or safer. Take note of the prices of fruits and vegetables on a per-kilogram or per-pound basis, so that if/when you buy at the street, you will know what a fair price is. I usually take pictures of the prices at a supermarket and show it to the street vendor if they try to rip me off.

Trivia from fellow travelers

Hydro-electric power in Leticia, Colombia: I met two Swedish university students who were going to work on a non-dam hydro-electric power plant as part of their thesis for their Master's program. The power was to be generated by the flow of the river – hence providing not that much power as compared to traditional hydroelectric power generated with a dam. However, it would avoid all the disadvantages that building a dam brings. Instead, a steel turbine was to be placed in the river. And unlike wind turbines, which have been accused of killing birds, no fish would die from this turbine. If a fish got caught in the flow, eventually it would just be able to flow out.

I met a girl from Spain who was in Colombia to study Biology. When I asked, "Why Colombia?" – she said that Colombia has the second greatest biodiversity on the planet. Brazil has the most.

I met some Swedish girls in Chile, who were there to study wine. When I asked, "Why Chile?" – they said Chile has the best wine. That was back in 2000. I am not sure where Chile stands today, and given climate change, I will not be surprised if one day, a place like London may produce the best wine from its vineyards.

According to an American farmer who had relocated to Ecuador, in Ecuador, goats and other animals are just mated or bred with that of their friends or neighbors. In the U.S., they are all bred with productivity or profit in mind. Consequently, only the best are bred - best in the sense of not just milk production but also flow of milk.

What started out as a casual conversation with my neighbor in Ecuador ended up stretching for about four hours, and I learned the following:

On meditation: The trick is not to focus on anything. Just be aware of the thoughts that are passing through your head. Over time, the thoughts will come slowly. Alternatively, as she experienced on one of her hiking expeditions, she was so exhausted, all she could do was to focus on putting one leg in front of another, one at a time. That, to her, was meditation.

Stomach and/or bladder issues are unresolved anger issues. It could include being angry with oneself. Note that she is not a medical doctor, so take the two preceding sentences however you would like to.

Lost in translation

When I was living in Guadalajara, every Sunday, I went to the Farmer's market to purchase my fruits, vegetables, and legumes for the week. Every week, I saw these 3 ladies: grandmother, mother, and daughter. Every week, we smiled and exchanged greetings. On Sunday, Aug 5th, 2018, the grandmother paused and said the following to me: *"Lo apreciamos mucho de corazon y nos caei muy bien."* I understood it enough to know that it was a good 'comment' to respond 'Igualmente,' which is 'likewise' in English. However, I knew that the grandmother knew that my Spanish was limited and yet, she stopped to tell me that. Her expression as she told me was full of emotion that I decided to ask them to type on my smartphone what it meant and the daughter obliged and typed it. Google translated it as: "We really appreciate it and we liked it very much." I sensed that was not a good translation at all, and later asked my bilingual friends what it meant, and their answers varied. I realized then, that even though what she was trying to convey to me was lost in translation; her emotions as she said it to me was not lost, because it meant more than words. I wish I could reproduce for you that moment that is etched in my mind – but I can't. Pictures can never do justice to what we actually see. Neither can words adequately convey our experience. We can only attempt.

On a lighter note

On my first morning in Vilcabamba, Ecuador, I took a walk to the downtown from my hostel. Along the way, I saw a lot of shit, and different kinds of shit. Shits of all shapes and sizes. Don't ask me why, but I tried to classify them. "This must be dog shit. I guess this might be horse shit? Shit! I don't know what shit, this is! Shit here! Shit there! Shit everywhere! Shit! This place is full of shit!!!"

PS: Though the above is true, I do not want to leave the impression that the whole town is like that. It is not. It just happened to be that way on the path that I took that day.

Holly was in Nepal in 2015 when a magnitude 8.1 earthquake hit. She recounted a story of her friend, who was also there at a restaurant when the aftershock hit. Her friend said that all the men just fled as quickly as possible, climbing over fences; leaving their wives or girlfriends behind. A new meaning to "All men for himself."

During the Gyeongbokgung palace tour in South Korea, I learned that the king's residence had no furniture, because of fear of the possibility of assassins hiding. As such, the king had no bed, too. He slept on the mattress with no bed. If a king can sleep without a bed, I don't understand why people gave me such a hard time for not having a bed.

Kindness

Many years ago, I took the train from California to Colorado. That night, as I was half asleep on my seat, I sensed a lady covering me gently with a blanket. It reminded me of what my mom used to do occasionally when I was a kid. In my drowsy state, I thought I was dreaming. When I woke up in the morning, there was indeed a blanket over me. I figured it must belong to the lady behind me; so I asked if it was hers, thanked her and returned it. She said with a gentle smile that she saw me crouching last night and figured a blanket might help. That incident made a certain Buddhist suggestion more meaningful — that one reflects upon the idea that all beings have, in one lifetime or another, been your mother.

June 27th, 2018, Guadalajara, Mexico: People have only asked me for money. No one has offered money to me voluntarily, until now. I was at the market, choosing some mangoes to purchase, when a lady came by and offered 20 pesos (about one U.S. dollar). I asked her why in Spanish, but

I did not understand her reply in Spanish. I politely said "*No gracias*." (No, thank you in Spanish.) A couple of weeks earlier, I was at the supermarket, Soriana Súper. While searching my pockets for 5 pesos to store my bag at the locker, a girl came by and offered me her 5 pesos with a pleasant smile. I am lucky to be blessed by the encounters of some very kind people.

Panama, March 2016: I met an American Palestinian lady. She recounted to me how one day while hiking in Panama, she took the wrong road and ended up in the wrong place. A Panamanian family offered her water and food. She found out that the lady's son walks three hours every day for work in the town. That's three hours, one way. She was so moved by it that she bought for him a bicycle out of her limited budget. She said, "I don't have much, but I certainly have more than they have."

Inflation without borders

When I was in Mexico, I had the opportunity to talk to a guy who used to work illegally in the U.S. There were anywhere between 20 to 30 people, including a pregnant woman, who made the trip to the U.S. illegally with him. It was supposed to take a day but the guide lost his way and it took an extra day instead. Along the way, he saw at least one dead body, and there were rattlesnakes. He was able to get a fake ID and eventually worked as a forklift driver in a packaging factory. In 2005, he was earning $18/hour in that job. After the financial crisis, job opportunities disappeared and he consequently returned to Mexico.

He disclosed the following: An illegal worker entering the U.S. from Mexico in 1997 had to pay $1,000 USD. In 2001, he paid $3,000 USD. In 2016, he thought it was about $10,000 USD. Inflation does not discriminate. Everyone gets dinged.

Courage

Luis is an 11-year-old kid in Ajijic, Mexico. The first time I encountered him, he was street vending with a pleasant smile. I stopped him and asked him in Spanish how much the blueberries were. He answered me in English. It was more expensive than usual, and it didn't look that good, either. So, I offered him the usual (lower) price I pay, but he declined with a nonchalant smile. He then continued walking with his good cheer. He formed an impression on me. I do not know why, but it is always the lowly blue-collar workers that have formed indelible impressions on me by the manner in which they carry themselves, despite the relatively poor remuneration they receive: A postwoman in Singapore, drenched in sweat from the heat and humidity, greeting me with a smile as she delivered a piece of registered mail; a bus driver in San Jose, California, looking me in the eye and saying "Good morning" as I boarded the bus at the crack of dawn; the staff at a restaurant in Cupertino, California, cleaning the plates with a quiet smile and serenity. These are the people that constantly remind me on how I should carry myself, despite the circumstances. I don't think I have succeeded yet in that goal, though.

One definition of 'good cheer is 'courage'. It takes courage to do what needs to be done day after day with a smile, despite whether it is appreciated or rewarded appropriately.

To all the 'Luis' out there – Courage!

Lessons from the screens

Many movies that are supposedly based on true stories are usually embellished. The science in some movies can be questionable too. Despite these and other shortcomings, I have found more than mere entertainment value in some movies. Consequently, over the years, I took notes on some movies where the conversations between characters were thought-provoking. In other cases, I learned more about some historical figures or events. Some movies prompted me to find out more about a person or event that was referenced in the movie. Most of the TV or movie transcript in this section has been chosen to complement the questions and thoughts explored in the preceding essays.

Disclaimer: There may be errors in the actual words quoted in the script or the names of the characters. However, it should not affect the meaning of what the conversation is trying to convey.

Seinfeld season 3, episode 4

Seinfeld: On my block, a lot of people walk their dogs, and I always see them walking along with their little poop bags, which to me is just the lowest function of human life. If aliens are watching this through telescopes, they're gonna think the dogs are the leaders. If you see two life forms, one of them is making a poop, the other one is carrying it for him, who would you assume was in charge?

Whatever Works

Thoughtful quotes from Boris Yellnikoff:

Oh, the human race. They've had to install automatic toilets in public restrooms, because people can't be entrusted to flush a toilet. Come on, flushing a toilet! They can't even flush a toilet!

It just shows what meaningless blind chance the universe is. Everybody schemes and dreams to meet the right person, and I jump out a window and land on her. That's why I can't say enough times, whatever love you can get and give, whatever happiness you can filch or provide, every temporary measure of grace, whatever works. And don't kid yourself, it's by no means all up to your own human ingenuity. A bigger part of your existence is luck than you'd like to admit.

Adaptation

Charlie: How come you looked so happy?
Donald: I loved Sarah, Charles. It was mine, that love. I owned it. Even Sarah didn't have the right to take it away. I can love whoever I want.
Charlie: But she thought you were pathetic.
Donald: That was her business, not mine. You are what you love, not what loves you. That's what I decided a long time ago.

My comment: Recall Question 4 and the essay "Love"? Isn't it better to derive all your joy from loving someone? In that way, you own it, and like Donald, you can be happy even when the love is unrequited.

Fiddler on the Roof

Background: Tevye, a Jewish milkman, has just decided to give Perchik permission to

become engaged to his daughter, Hodel.
Golde is his wife.

Tevye: Do you love me?

Golde: Do I what?

Tevye: Do you love me?

Golde: Do I love you?

With our daughters getting married

And this trouble in the town

You're upset, you're worn out

Go inside, go lie down!

Maybe it's indigestion

Tevye: Golde, I'm asking you a question...

Do you love me?

Golde: You're a fool

Tevye: I know...

But do you love me?

Golde: Do I love you?

For twenty-five years I've washed your clothes

Cooked your meals, cleaned your house

Given you children, milked the cow

After twenty-five years, why talk about love right now?

Tevye: Golde, The first time I met you Was on our wedding day

I was scared

Golde: I was shy

Tevye: I was nervous

Golde: So was I

Tevye: But my father and my mother Said we'd learn to love each other. And now I'm asking, Golde, Do you love me?

Golde: I'm your wife

Tevye: I know... But do you love me?

Golde: Do I love him? For twenty-five years I've lived with him

Fought him, starved with him Twenty-five years my bed is his

If that's not love, what is?

Tevye: Then you love me?

Golde: I suppose I do

Tevye: And I suppose I love you too

<u>The Princess and the Marine</u>

The princess: The Tree of Life is the symbol of Bahrain. It is the mystery that how the tree survives in the middle of the desert. And that's where the beauty is. It exists where it is not supposed to exist.

<u>The Inn of the Sixth Happiness</u>

The movie is based on a true story of Gladys Aylward, who wasn't qualified to be a missionary in China, so she worked and saved her way to China.

Handing a Chinese girl to her father, Gladys says “Here, the next time you want her feet bound, bind them yourself, not the woman, and you listen to her screams.”

Gladys: Yang says everyone in China wishes you the five happiness: wealth, longevity, good health, virtue and

Jeannie Lawson: And a peaceful death in old age, yes.

Gladys Aylward: But he didn't mention any more. What is the sixth happiness?

Jeannie Lawson: That you must find out for yourself. Each person must find out in his heart what the sixth happiness is.

Captain Lin Nan: You are beautiful.

Gladys: Once in their life, every woman should have that said to her. I am glad you said it.

Gladys: Marriage for some people never happens, no matter where they are.

<u>The Laws of Thermodynamics</u>

This is a Spanish movie about an astrophysicist, Manel, who is obsessed with the idea that the permanent universal laws dictate our daily life. He works as a teacher assistant to Professor Amat. Eva is his friend's girlfriend.

The paragraphs below are a consolidated summary of the various dialogs in the movie:

The law of gravity or attraction of bodies. A body's gravity depends on its mass, which we mustn't identify by its weight, rather by the amount of attractive material. If we multiply her attractive mass by the speed of light squared, we get an immeasurable amount of energy. Gravity is a powerful force when it comes to attracting bodies to each other. But it stops being one once they've already been brought together.

Life is probably just a consequence of how atoms organize themselves, another step in the evolution of complex systems. The initial conditions within a system are what determine its evolution.

Most people would say that strong nuclear force is love because it makes particles inseparable. But more careful analysis demonstrates that it's actually more of a dependence.

But this phenomenon is merely a consequence of the deepest and most terrifying truth presented by quantum physics: wave-particle duality. At the exact moment you observe the particle, the cloud and the rest of the possibilities disappear. The particle stops behaving like a wave and it's really doing what you see. They say quantum physics put an end to scientific determinism.

Probability, let's repeat, is just as determinant over time as the most exact of all laws. It's infallible. And even worse, it leaves you with no weapons to fight it. In the end, probability always puts you in your place.

Why do you think entropy always marks the worst direction possible? Because the chances of things turning out the way you want are ridiculous compared to the chances they won't.

The chances of the other particles being where you want them to be will always be extremely small.

At one time all of the bodies in the universe were very close, squeezed together in the form of pure energy.

Manel to a student: The second law of thermodynamics explains why a glass you drop smashes into pieces on the floor but if you drop the pieces they don't form a glass. It explains why machines stop working if you don't use them, why sand castles never last and why we always end up forgetting everything. It explains why what you wanted to do becomes the mess you end up making and why your girlfriend gets bored with you and finds someone else. It even explains why we can't go back in time and fix the things we screwed up with her. It explains practically everything you do wrong. Because it applies to all systems, starting with the universe itself and ending with your own life and the shitty social system you're wasting away in.

My note: According to Wikipedia: Quantum entanglement is a physical phenomenon that occurs when pairs or groups of particles are generated, interact, or share spatial proximity in ways such that
the quantum state of each particle cannot be described independently of the state of the others, even when the particles are separated by a large distance.

Eva to Manel, in an attempt to get Manel to get out of his rut: That law of quantum entanglement. You say that if you change the state of one particle, it changes the state of the other one too, right? Then if you change yourself to a more positive state, if you take care of yourself and surround yourself with good vibes, then maybe Elena won't be as happy and she'll start missing you.

Professor Amat to Manel: You know that the electromagnetic field passes through walls.

Oblivion

The protagonist, Jack Harper's, monologue: The questions I ask, she doesn't; the things I wonder about, she won't.

My comment: This seems to be the recurring theme among protagonists. A solitary soul wondering or questioning what the masses don't. Whether it is the movie Matrix, Fight Club, or Oblivion, there is relentless restlessness within the protagonists that things are not as what they appear; that there is something more. These protagonists are usually helped in their enlightenment process by someone who recognizes the potential in them.

<u>An Education</u>

Jenny Mellor: That is it with our lives. It is so easy to fall asleep when there is nothing to keep you awake.

<u>Jack Reacher</u>

Jack Reacher: Would you tell me what you see?

Helen: I see the same... things I see every day.

Jack Reacher: Well, imagine you've never seen it. Imagine you've spent your whole life in other parts of the world being told every day you're defending freedom. And finally, you decide you've had enough. Time to see what you've given up your whole life for. Maybe get some of that freedom for yourself. Look at the people. Now, tell me which ones are free. Free from debt. Anxiety. Stress. Fear. Failure. Indignity. Betrayal. How many wish that they were born knowing what they know now? Ask yourself how many would do things the same way over again? And how many would live their lives like me."

The following quote by the character Jack Reacher is not from the movie but from the novel 'Bad Luck and Trouble' by Lee Child:

"Slippery slope. I carry a spare shirt, pretty soon I'm carrying spare pants. Then I'd need a suitcase. Next thing I know, I've got a house and a car and a savings plan, and I'm filling out all kinds of forms."

Men in Black

Edwards: Why the big secret? People are smart. They can handle it.

Kay: A person is smart. People are dumb, panicky, dangerous animals, and you know it. Fifteen hundred years ago, everybody knew the Earth was the center of the universe. Five hundred years ago, everybody knew the Earth was flat, and fifteen minutes ago, you knew that humans were alone on this planet. Imagine what you'll know tomorrow.

<u>True Detective</u>

Maggie Hart, Marty's wife, contrasts her husband and Rust (Marty's partner) as follows:

Rust knew exactly who he was, and there was no talking him out of it. You know, Marty's single big problem was that he never really knew himself, so he never really knew what to want.

Some quotes from Rust:

Maybe the honorable thing for our species to do is deny our programming, stop reproducing, walk hand in hand into extinction, one last midnight - brothers and sisters opting out of a raw deal.

The world needs bad men. We keep the other bad men from the door.

Death created time to grow the things that it would kill.

If the only thing keeping a person decent is the expectation of divine reward, then, brother, that person is a piece of shit.

Just gotta look a man in his eyes. It's all there. Everybody wears their hunger and their haunt, you know?

You know, people that give me advice, I reckon they're talking to themselves.

<u>First Reformed</u>

Reverend Ernst Toller: Courage is the solution to despair.

Reverend Jeffers: We tend to think that anxiety and worry are simply an indication of how wise we are, yet it is a much better indication of how wicked we are. Fretting arises from our determination to have our own way. Our Lord never worried and was never anxious. Because His purpose was to accomplish not his own plans.

Noah

Background: In the movie, Noah believes he needs to murder his two granddaughters to fulfill God's will. Although there is no such indication of this in the Bible, it is a good scene to illustrate the point of following our conscience instead of cowardly hiding behind excuses such as "It is God's will" or "It is in the Holy Book." Naameh is Noah's wife and 'Him" and "He" below refers to God.

Naameh: I have to know. Why did you spare them?

Noah: I looked down at those two little girls and all I had in my heart was love.

Naameh: Then why are you alone, Noah? Why are you separated to your family?

Noah: Because I failed Him, and I failed all of you.

Naameh: Did you? He chose you for a reason, Noah. He showed you the wickedness of Man and knew you would not look away. And you saw goodness too. The choice was put in your hands because he put it there. He asked you to decide if we were worth saving. And you chose mercy. You chose love. He has given us a second chance. Be a father, be a grandfather. Help us to do better this time. Help us start again.

My comment: "They show that the requirements of the law are written on their hearts, their consciences also bearing witness, and their thoughts sometimes accusing them and at other times even defending them." (Romans 2:15)

God's Not Dead 2

Background of characters: Mr. Endler is the defense attorney and Mr. Kane is the prosecutor. Lee Strobel and James Wallace are real-life characters who play the role of trial witnesses in this movie.

Mr. Endler: Can you help me prove the existence of Jesus Christ?

Lee Strobel: Absolutely, beyond any reasonable doubt.

Mr. Endler: How so?

Lee Strobel: Actually, this court already affirmed it when we were called into session and the date was given. Our calendar has been split between B.C. and A.D. based on the birth of Jesus, which is quite a feat if he never existed. Beyond that, historian Gary Habermas lists 39 ancient sources for Jesus, from which he enumerates more than 100 reported facts about his life, teachings, crucifixion, and resurrection. In fact, the historical evidence for Jesus' execution is so strong that one of the most famous New Testament scholars in the world, Gerd Ludemann of Germany, said, "Jesus' death as a consequence of crucifixion is indisputable." Now, there are very few facts in ancient history that a critical historian like Gerd Ludemann will say is indisputable. One of them is the execution of Jesus Christ.

Mr. Endler: Forgive me, but you're a believer, are you not? A Bible-believing Christian?

Lee Strobel: Guilty as charged.

Mr. Endler: So, wouldn't this tend to inflate your estimate of the probability that Jesus existed?

Lee Strobel: No, because we don't need to inflate it. We can reconstruct the basic facts about Jesus just from non-Christian sources outside the Bible. And Gerd Ludemann is an atheist. In other words, we can prove the existence of Jesus solely by using sources that have absolutely no sympathy toward Christianity. As the agnostic historian, Bart Ehrman, says, "Jesus did exist, whether we like it or not." I put it this way: Denying the existence of Jesus doesn't make him go away. It merely proves that no amount of evidence will convince you.

Mr. Endler: Thank you. No further questions, Your Honor.

Mr. Endler: Would you state your name and experience for the record?

James Wallace: My name is James Warner Wallace. I'm a retired homicide detective from Los Angeles County.

Mr. Endler: And are you the author of the book, "Cold Case Christianity"?

James Wallace: Yes, I am.

Mr. Endler Can you share the subtitle of the book with the court, please?

James Wallace: "A Homicide Detective Investigates the Claims of the Gospels."

Mr. Endler: Would I be correct in saying that your duties as a homicide detective include investigating cold case homicides?

James Wallace: Yes, that is and was my expertise.

Mr. Endler: Don't most of those cases get solved with DNA evidence?

Mr. Kane: Objection, leading. And counsel is testifying again, Your Honor.

Mr. Endler: I'll rephrase. How many of your cold cases were solved through the use of DNA evidence?

James Wallace: None. Not one. That's often popular on TV, but our departments never had the good fortune of solving a cold case with DNA.

Mr. Endler Well, how do most of these cases get solved?

James Wallace: Often by examining eyewitness claims, witness claims that were made many years earlier, even though often our witnesses are now deceased.

Mr. Endler: Forgive my ignorance, Mr. Wallace, but how is that possible?

James Wallace: Well, we have a number of techniques we can use to test the reliability of an eyewitness, including something called forensic statement analysis. That's a discipline where we scrutinize the statements of eyewitnesses and looking at what they choose to minimize, what they choose to emphasize, what they omit altogether, how they expand time or contract time. And when we examine these kinds of eyewitness accounts, we can usually tell who's lying, and who's telling the truth, and even who the guilty party is.

Mr. Endler: And did you apply this skill set anytime outside of your official capacity?

James Wallace: Yes, I applied my expertise to the death of Jesus at the hands of the Romans, and I actually looked at the gospels as I would any other set of forensic statements. Within a matter of months, I determined that the four gospels, written from different perspectives, contained the eyewitness accounts about the life, ministry, death, and resurrection of Jesus.

Mr. Endler: And did you consider that the four accounts might be part of a conspiracy, designed to promote belief in a fledgling faith?

James Wallace: Yeah, you have to consider conspiracies when assessing eyewitness accounts, but successful conspiracies typically involve the fewest number of people. It's a lot easier for 2 people to lie and keep a secret than it is for 20. And that's really the problem with the conspiracy theories related to the apostles in the 1st century. There are just far too many of them trying to hold this conspiracy for far too long a period of time. And far worse, they're experiencing pressure like no other, unimaginable pressure. Every one of these folks was tortured and died for what they claimed to see, and none of them ever recanted their story. So, the idea that this is a conspiracy in the 1st century is just really unreasonable. Instead, what I see in the gospels is something I call unintended eyewitness support statement.

Mr. Endler: What's an unintended eyewitness support statement?

James Wallace: If I can borrow your Bible? Let me go to the Gospel of Matthew for an example of this. I'll start with a passage in which Jesus is in front of Caiaphas at a hearing. It says here, "Then they spit in his face "and struck him with their fists."Others slapped him and said, 'Prophesy to us, Christ. Who hit you?'" Now, that seems like a very simple request, given that the people who hit him are standing right in front of him. This makes no sense. Why would it be prophecy to be able to tell you who hit you? But it's not until you read Luke that you get an answer to this. He says, "The men who were guarding Jesus "began mocking and beating him." They blindfolded him and demanded, 'Prophesy, who hit you?'" So, now we know why this was a challenge, 'cause Luke tells us the thing that Matthew left out, that he was actually blindfolded at the time this took place. This is very common, this kind of unintentional eyewitness support that fills in a detail that the first witness left out. After years of scrutinizing these gospels using the template that I use to determine if an eyewitness is reliable, I concluded that the four gospels in this book contained the reliable accounts of the actual words of Jesus.

Mr. Endler: And that's to include the statements quoted by Ms. Wesley in her class?

James Wallace: Absolutely.

Mr. Endler: Thank you, Detective. Your witness.

Mr. Kane: Detective Wallace, I'm not gonna try to match biblical knowledge with you. But isn't it true that these gospel accounts vary widely in what they say, that there are numerous discrepancies between these accounts?

James Wallace: Absolutely, but that's exactly what we should expect.

Mr. Kane: I don't quite understand that.

James Wallace: Well, reliable eyewitness accounts always differ slightly in the way they recall the story. They're coming to it from different geographic perspectives, their history, even where they are located in the room. When I examined the gospels, I was trying to determine if these were accurate, reliable accounts, in spite of any differences there might be between the accounts.

Mr. Kane: Ah, and as a devout Christian, you feel you succeeded?

James Wallace: Ah, Mr. Kane. I think you misunderstand me. When I began this study, I was a devout atheist. I began examining the gospels as a committed skeptic, not as a believer. You see, I wasn't raised in a Christian environment, although I do think I have an unusually high regard for the value of evidence. I'm not a Christian because I was raised that way or because I hoped it would satisfy some need or accomplish some goal. I'm simply a Christian because it's evidentially true.

Devil

You're never going to get these people to see themselves as they really are, 'cause it's the lies that we tell ourselves, they introduce us to him.

My comment: ‘him’ refers to the devil.

Doomsday Book

This is a Korean sci-fi movie with three stories. The second story titled Heavenly Creatures is about a robot reaching Nirvana. Below are selected conversations in English.

A monk: I learned that all awakened beings in this world are Buddha, and you have attained the highest point among us all. But they deem you defective and order a recall.

Robot: To perceive is to distinguish, merely a classification of knowing. While all living creatures share the same inherent nature, perception is what classifies one as Buddha and another as machine. We mistake perception as permanent truth and such delusions cause us pain.

Robot Company's President: People often see science as a mere instrument to mankind. A subservient aid to do its bidding, like some genie in a lamp. But each scientific advancement man utilizes is conversely changing man himself. Even before we realize it. When the first man wielded that wooden stick, the stick was also wielding him. Man has always been marginalized by class, capital and labor. And now we will be marginalized by a monster we created. Creator, at the will of his own creation! Understand? All creators face the dilemma that they've created a monster. But every problem has a solution.

The human brain has not evolved since the dissemination of computers, left only with basic arithmetic functions. What is the telephone number for this temple?

My comment: I wonder how many of us can remember important telephone numbers once they are saved onto our smartphones? The more we outsource our abilities to computers, the more we will be rendered useless unless we utilize our abilities in other meaningful activities.

Robot: I know I am without desire or compulsion, in the past, present, and future. I have learned that this is as the teachings of Buddha.

<u>Bokeh</u>

Two quotes by the character Nils:

1. The World is the world. You cannot fault it for not behaving in the way you think it should.

2. They say that God’s one and only voice is silence. He just must have more to say these days.

Dragonfly

Sister Madeline: “Talk to an anesthesiologist. They'll tell you. There are 100 steps on the ladder of consciousness between being fully alert and being dead. To put a patient under, they bring them down only to the 10th rung. Beneath that is a descending gray-scale, like the depths of an ocean no one has explored.”

(Patient is a female, who attempted to commit suicide)

Patient: Why did you do this to me?

Dr. Joe Darrow: Do what to you?

Patient: Bring me back.

Dr. Joe Darrow: Where were you going?

Patient: Someplace better.

Dr. Joe Darrow: Is that right?

Patient: I'll do it again, too. It's all I want now.

Dr. Joe Darrow: Well, unfortunately, your heart disagrees. It's waged quite a battle tonight.

Patient: No one knows my heart.

Dr. Joe Darrow: Maybe that's why it's still beating- to give somebody a chance to. Let me tell you about that better place you think you're going to. You better be damn sure it's there. 'Cause crappy as this place is, it's all there is. So go ahead. Be my guest. But when you never wake up again, don't say I didn't warn you.

The Men Who Stare At Goats

Lyn Cassady: Bob, have you ever heard of "Optimum Trajectory"?

Bob: What?

Lyn Cassady: "Optimum trajectory."

Your life is like a river. And if you're aiming for a goal that isn't your destiny, you'll always gonna be swimming against the current. Young Gandhi wants to be a stock-car driver? It's not gonna happen. Little Anne Frank wants to be a high school teacher. Tough titty, Anne. That's not your destiny. But you will go on to move the hearts and minds of millions. Find out what your destiny is, and the river will carry you. Now, sometimes events in life give an individual clues as to where their destiny lies. Like those little doodles you just happened to draw?

(Lyn Cassady unbuttons his shirt to reveal a tattoo of the Ajna chakra on his chest)

It's the Ajna chakra, the third eye. The symbol of the Jedi. When I saw that you're drawing it, well, the Universe gives you clues like that, you don't ignore it. You're meant to be here with me, Bob.

I, Origins

Background: Dr. Ian Grey is a scientist who believes in data. Sofi, a model, is Ian’s girlfriend and Karen is his laboratory partner.

Sofi: Do you know the story of the Phasianidae?

Ian: The... No, what's that?

Sofi: It's a bird that experiences all of time in one instant. And she sings the song of love and anger and fear and joy and sadness all at once. And this bird... when she meets the love of her life... is both happy and sad. Happy because she sees that for him it is the beginning, and sad because she knows it is already over.

Sofi: How many senses do worms have?

Ian: They have two. Smell and touch. Why?

Sofi: So... they live without any ability to see or even know about light, right? The notion of light to them is unimaginable.

Ian: Yeah.

Sofi: But we humans... we know that light exists. All around them... right on top of them... they cannot sense it. But with a little mutation, they do. Right?

Ian: Correct.

Sofi: So... Doctor Eye... perhaps some humans, rare humans... have mutated to have another sense. A spirit sense. And can perceive a world that is right on top of us... everywhere. Just like the light on these worms.

Ian: I don't believe in luck. I do believe we've known each other since forever, though.

Sofi: Really?

Ian: Yeah. You know how? When the Big Bang happened, all the atoms in the universe, they were all smashed together into one little dot that exploded outward. So my atoms and your atoms were certainly together then, and, who knows, probably smashed together several times in the last 13.7 billion years. So my atoms have known your atoms and they've always known your atoms. My atoms have always loved your atoms.

Priya Varma: You know a scientist once asked the Dalai Lama, "What would you do if something scientific disproved your religious beliefs?" And he said, after much thought, "I would look at all the papers. I'd take a look at all the research and really try to understand things. And in the end, if it was clear that the scientific evidence disproved my spiritual beliefs, I would change my beliefs."

Ian: That's a good answer.

Priya Varma: Ian... what would you do if something spiritual disproved your scientific beliefs?

Karen: If I drop this phone a thousand times, a million times... and one time, it doesn't fall... just once, it hovers in the air. That is an error that's worth looking at.

Ian: You know we could be looking forever and find nothing.

Karen: Turning over rocks and finding nothing is progress.

1898, Our Last Men in the Philippines (Spanish title: 1898, Los últimos de Filipinas)

For about four centuries, the Philippines were under Spain. This film, based on true events, recounts the final days of the Spanish Empire's last colony in the Philippines. Fifty-four Spanish soldiers were sent to reclaim the village of Baler. While they are under siege, they are informed, more than once, that the war was over for Spain. However, Lt. Martín Cerezo refuses to believe. For one, he found it hard to believe that Spain would have sold the Philippines to the United States for the sum of $20 million. Consequently, he ordered his men to continue fighting and it continued for six more months, despite soldiers dying and deserting. This is yet another story that reflects how willfully blind people can get during times of war.

Not in the movie: Martín Cerezo later published a memoir, "El Sitio de Baler", where he gave his reasons for holding out:

"It would be somewhat difficult for me to explain, principally, I believe through mistrust and obstinacy. Then also on account of a certain kind of auto-suggestion that we ought not for any reason surrender because of national enthusiasm, without doubt influenced by the attractive illusion of glory and on account of the suffering and treasury of sacrifice and heroism and that by surrender, we would be putting an unworthy end to it all."

Food for thought: Lt. Martin Cerezo is not the only crackpot to have kept fighting long after a war ended. Hiroo Onoda, a Japanese soldier, spent 29 years holding out in the Philippines after the war ended, until his former commander flew from Japan to formally relieve him from duty. How often to justify the continuation of war, do we hear “leaders” saying that to stop fighting and returning will be a disservice to the soldiers who have died in the war? If you invested thousands of dollars in an investment, but it went south and you lost the money, will you continue to inject more money into that investment? If we don’t do it with money, why do we do it with lives? They say nothing is certain but death and taxes. Well, you can add war to that. There will always be at least one idiot somewhere who will find a reason to keep fighting.

Chernobyl, season 1, episode 4

The Chernobyl disaster resulted in soldiers getting villages to evacuate. Below is what an old lady tells a soldier when commanded by him to leave:

Lady: I'm 82. I've lived here my whole life. Right here, that house, this place. What do I care about safe?

Soldier: I have a job. Don't cause trouble.

Lady: Trouble? You're not the first soldier to stand here with a gun. When I was 12, the revolution came. Czar's men. Then Bolsheviks. Boys like you marching in lines. They told us to leave. *No*. Then there was Stalin and his famine, the Holodomor. My parents died. Two of my sisters died. They told the rest of us to leave. *No*. Then the Great War. German boys. Russian boys. More soldiers, more famine, more bodies.

My brothers never came home. But I stayed, and I'm still here. After all that I have seen so I should leave now, because of something I cannot see at all? *No.*

Chernobyl, season 1, episode 5

Colonel Shcherbina: Do you know anything about this town, Chernobyl?

Professor Legasov: Not really, no.

Colonel Shcherbina: It was mostly Jews and Poles. The Jews were killed in pogroms, and Stalin forced the Poles out. And then the Nazis came and killed whoever was left. But after the war, people came to live here anyway. They knew the ground under their feet was soaked in blood, but they didn't care. Dead Jews, dead Poles. But not them. No one ever thinks it's going to happen to them. And here we are.

STEPASHIN: Professor Legasov, if you mean to suggest the Soviet State is somehow responsible for what happened, then I must warn you, you are treading on dangerous ground.

Professor Legasov: I've already trod on dangerous ground. We're on dangerous ground right now, because of our secrets and our lies. They're practically what define us. When the truth offends, we lie and lie until we can no longer remember it is even there. But it is still there. Every lie we tell incurs a debt to the truth. Sooner or later, that debt is paid. That is how an RBMK reactor core explodes. Lies.

Professor Legasov’s monologue: To be a scientist is to be naive. We are so focused on our search for truth, we fail to consider how few actually want us to find it. But it is always there, whether we see it or not, whether we choose to or not. The truth doesn't care about our needs or wants. It doesn't care about our governments, our ideologies, our religions. It will lie in wait for all time. And this, at last, is the gift of Chernobyl. Where I once would fear the cost of truth, now I only ask: What is the cost of lies?

Albert Einstein - How I See the World

This is a documentary on physicist Albert Einstein. My notes from the movie:

Einstein was a pacifist and an admirer of Gandhi's passive resistance. The U.S. government gathered top American and exiled European scientists, but Einstein was excluded because he was considered a national security risk. On March 25th, 1945; he wrote a second letter to the president to indicate that if the atom bomb was actually used, the consequences would be great. FDR died before the letter was opened. Scientists tried to persuade the government not to drop the bomb. Einstein regretted writing the first letter to Roosevelt: "I could burn my fingers that I wrote that first letter to President Roosevelt." The first letter recommended that atom bombs be made.

Ancient Chinese saying: "It is impossible to know the results of your actions."

$E = mc^2$ was the basic theoretical formulation of nuclear fission.

A nuclear weapon is the cheapest way to kill people.

Some quotes from Einstein:

Our spirit must conquer technology.

The greatest experience we can have is the mysterious.

I want to go when I am ready, and I will do it in an elegant way.

What does a fish know about the water in which he swims all his life?

Hiroshima

Professor Leo Szilard, a Jew from Hungary, was the one who convinced Einstein to write the letter to Roosevelt, to look into an atomic bomb. The Manhattan Project was formed, with about 200,000 people and $2 billion spent over three years. When Roosevelt died, he was succeeded by Harry Truman. Kyoto was one of the first suggested targets for the bomb. However, since Kyoto was to Japan what Rome was to Europe, they decided against it. On June 1st,

1945, it was decided unanimously to use the bomb. On Aug 8th, 1945, the bomb was dropped in Hiroshima.

Beyond Rangoon

Student leader, U Aung Ko: We are taught that suffering is the only promise life makes - so that when happiness comes it is a precious gift, and it is only for a brief time.

What I learned from the movie:

People pay money to set birds free, but little do they know that the bird flies back to the cage because it knows no other world than the cage.

Burma was under military dictatorship. But every man spends some time as a monk.

When your mind is quiet, it receives wisdom.

Karen guerillas had been fighting for more than 40 years. Many people were killed in the democracy movement. Although in 1990, Aung's party won - the military refused to give power.

Aung authored the book *Freedom From Fear.*

Billions

A motivational speech from season 1, episode 6, given by Axelrod to his staff after one of their colleagues is arrested:

Today, we are standing at the precipice. Today is one day after. The day after Pearl Harbor, everybody knew a Japanese invasion would be coming. Air raid wardens. Anti-aircraft artillery. Cities blacked out. Mothers and fathers staying by the door with baseball bats and kitchen knives, bellies full of fear of the invading hordes. But everyone was wrong. What happened on American soil next? Nothing. That's right. The invasion never came. Turned out Pearl Harbor was the best those sneak attacking Motherf*ckers had. What came next was a war that unleashed the might of America. What came next was a victory that left us as the most powerful nation on Earth. This company will not wait for an uncertain future. We will make our own future! We will fight back hard. We will mobilize the war machine. And those who would try to bring down our house will see their own houses fall!

Borgen

This is a Danish television series, where the protagonist, Birgitte Nyborg, becomes the first female prime minister of Denmark.

Birgitte Nyborg: Elna Munch, Helga Larsen, Karen Ankersted, Mathilde Malling Hauschultz. I hope we all know these names. These are four women who were the first of their gender to gain a seat in Parliament in 1918, and thus ended the Parliament debate about whether women are cut out to be politicians. To all those who wish to debate whether women should enter politics on equal terms with men and ultimately make Prime Minister, I can only say: You're 100 years behind.

(People around the room smile)

So many insignificant topics have been discussed. Did any of you really believe I intended to resign and become a housewife? You must not know me at all, then. I very much want to end all these foolish discussions. Today, the last part of the government reform package was passed. We've shown you where we want to take Denmark. I'm very pleased and proud of that. That's why I'm going to let the Danish voters decide. Not what gender the prime minister should be, but whom they feel is the best prime minister for Denmark.

<u>Whiskey Tango Foxtrot</u>

Background: Kim Baker is the embedded reporter who interviews Coughlin, a Marine in Afghanistan. Coughlin makes an offhand comment, which Kim quotes. Coughlin is subsequently transferred to a new unit where he gets his legs blown off. Kim, feeling guilty, pays him a visit in the U.S.

Coughlin: Ma'am, I lost my legs because of an IED, not because of you.

Kim: I appreciate that. But if I hadn't quoted you, you wouldn't have been transferred. No, really, you can say whatever you want to me. That's why I'm here.

Coughlin: OK, then let's say you're right. It's still not 'cause of you, ma'am. Some 12-year old hadji had to plant that bomb. And hell, if Bin Laden's parents hadn't gotten divorced, maybe none of us would have been in this damn to begin with. And the Taliban, they wouldn't have even been there for UBL, if Breznev hadn't gone and fouled up Afghanistan in the first place. And the British Empire. Oh, and Kim Baker.

Kim: OK, I deserved that.

Coughlin: Goddam! When you got no legs, everyone takes everything so serious! There's only so much any of us have any control of, good or bad. If you didn't learn that in Afghanistan, you were not paying attention. I mean, ma'am, Kim, you gotta move on. You're giving yourself way too much credit. You embrace the suck, you move the f*ck forward. What other f*cking choice do we have?

<u>Kon-Tiki</u>

This movie is based on a true story. 'Kon-Tiki' is the name of the balsa wood raft that Norwegian Thor Heyerdahl travels on from Peru to Polynesia in 1947. His objective: To prove that people from South America settled in Polynesia, instead of people from Asia. The experts at that time believed the latter. Even when many scoffed his idea on crossing the Pacific Ocean on a raft, and later, when his own crew eventually began to have doubts, Thor persevered in his faith. He believed that, just like the Peruvians about 1500 years ago, he too with the help of the ocean's currents and the stars would be able to cross the Pacific Ocean.

Side note: Some scientists refused to believe that the incredible voyage had actually taken place until a documentary film about the expedition was released. Thor Heyerdahl's documentary about the journey won an Oscar in 1951. His book on the expedition was translated into 70 languages and has sold over 50 million copies. In his 1997 memoir, "In the Footsteps of Adam," he frequently makes the point that academic specialists often fail to see the forest for the trees.

Recall the first essay "Faith? In that essay, Blondin was fortunate to have at least one person who had faith in him. In Thor's case, when things became difficult, everyone seemed to lose their faith in him. It is bad when no one has faith in you. It is worse when you don't have faith in yourself. Thor persevered in his faith. It is not always easy to trust yourself when all men doubt you.

Some quotes from Thor Heyerdahl:

The more I do and the more I see, the more I realize the shocking extent of ignorance that exists among the scholarly circles that call themselves authorities and pretend to have a monopoly of all knowledge,

We have always been taught that navigation is the result of civilization, but modern archeology has demonstrated very clearly that this is not so.

A civilized nation can have no enemies, and one cannot draw a line across a map, a line that doesn't even exist in nature, and say that the ugly enemy lives on the one side, and good friends live on the other.

One learns more from listening than speaking. And both the wind and the people who continue to live close to nature still have much to tell us which we cannot hear within university walls.

Progress can today be defined as man`s ability to complicate simplicity.

It is progress when a centuries-old oak is cut down to give space for a road sign.

In my experience, it is rarer to find a really happy person in a circle of millionaires than among vagabonds.

Moneyball

The book and movie 'Moneyball' revealed that the traditional yardsticks of success for players and teams are fatally flawed. The data has been there for ages, but nobody mined it to harness it to their advantage. The team with the most money seemed to be winning until Billy Beane – the general manager for the Oakland Athletics -- and

Paul DePodesta came along. In a way, Billy had no choice, because he had the second-lowest payroll in baseball. By focusing on what really matters to win and going after abilities that are dramatically underpriced in relation to other abilities, the Oakland Athletics succeeded in breaking the American League record for consecutive wins. Instead of focusing on buying players; they switched to focusing on buying wins. You buy wins by buying runs, which is grossly undervalued. They succeeded in reinventing a system that has been working for years. They redefined whatever everybody thought they knew about baseball.

Reminder to me: Don't follow the crowd. Drill down to find out what really matters.

Secretariat

The movie is based on the famous American racehorse, Secretariat. It was assumed that a horse is either good at endurance or speed but not both. Secretariat revealed the flaw in that assumption.

Cliffy

This is a telemovie based on a true story. Australian farmer Cliff Young was 61 years old, a vegetarian, a teetotaler, and a virgin when he announced he wanted to take part in the Sydney to Melbourne race. He became a laughingstock because he had never run a marathon before. While other contestants were younger, had run similar races before and were running with ‘proper’ running shoes sponsored by famous brands, Cliffy ran with his gumboots. Many professionals commented that his technique was considered “incorrect” because instead of running, he traipsed along with a leisurely shuffle. But Cliffy won first place, breaking the race record by 9 hours! Later, people who studied his running technique called it the ”Young Shuffle,” which has since been adopted by some ultra-marathon runners because it expends less energy.

Louis Pasteur

Louis Pasteur was not a doctor but a chemist. At that time, it was difficult for people, including the scientific community, to accept that microbes could kill humans. How could a microscopic thing kill something that is so many times bigger? The medical establishment ridiculed him. But Pasteur persisted in trying to prove that airborne microbes were the cause of disease.

<u>Scorpion season 2, episode 8</u>

Background: Walter is a genius with an IQ of 197; Megan is Walter's sister. Paige is a single mom, and Toby is a genius behavioral psychiatrist.

Walter: Can you explain Megan's condition as it stands?

Toby: She has a bacterial infection in her lungs. A pneumonia.

Walter: Why is that?

Toby: She has scarred, damaged lungs.

Walter: Why?

Toby: She's inhaled small amounts of food and saliva that, over time, have damaged her lungs.

Walter: Mm-hmm. Why is that happening?

Toby: Uh, she can't swallow very well because of the MS.

Walter: Uh, explain.

Toby: The MS damaged some nerves in her brain, probably her medulla.

Walter: How come?

Toby: Her own immune system attacked the myelin sheaths around the nerves.

Walter: Thank you, Toby. (clicks phone off) See? We know everything we need to know.

Paige: (clicks phone on) Toby... why is her own body attacking her nerves?

Toby: You know, we don't know.

Spectral

This is a sci-fi movie and the under-mentioned are quotes from the character Mark Clyne, a DARPA engineer.

What do you think it is?

Something no one's thought of yet.

Your technician's job is to find glitches, so, he sees glitches. Your job is to find the enemy, so, you see the enemy. Locals believe in spirits, so they see spirits. Everyone is biased, in one way or another.

So my answer to you right now is that we lack data to support any theory.

I know what they are. We think we're seeing things. We think it can't be real, but it kills. So, it is real. It's something. It's not light, it's not shadow, or some trick of the mind.

Pass through walls, check. Outside the visible spectrum, check. Kills to the touch, check.

Comstock. He was under a ceramic bathtub, is that right? Tank armor. It couldn't pass through tank armor. M1 Abrams tank armor, that's ceramic plating everywhere. It cannot pass through ceramic. You know what that means?

It means this stuff isn't natural. Someone made it. It's man-made.

Man-made how? Okay. You have solid, liquid, gas. Lava can turn into rock.

Ice can turn into water. Metals can melt. These are natural states. But there are unnatural states. Artificial states, man-made states. Condensate. Bose-Einstein condensate. A state of matter that was predicted by Nath Bose and Albert Einstein. It has some very unusual properties. It can be slowed down by iron filings. It cannot pass through ceramic, but it can pass through walls. It's so cold it will kill you instantly on contact. It can do everything we've been seeing here.

To create Bose-Einstein condensate, you need power, and you need a lot of it.

Another Earth

Rhoda Williams: You know that story of the Russian cosmonaut? So, the cosmonaut, he's the first man ever to go into space. Right? The Russians beat the Americans. So he goes up in this big spaceship, but the only habitable part of it's very small. So the cosmonaut's in there, and he's got this portal window, and he's looking out of it, and he sees the curvature of the Earth for the first time. I mean, the first man to ever look at the planet he's from. And he's lost in that moment. And all of a sudden this strange ticking begins coming out of the dashboard. Rips out the control panel, right? Takes out his tools, trying to find the sound, trying to stop the sound. But he can't find it. He can't stop it. It keeps going. Few hours into this, begins to feel like torture. A few days go by with this sound, and he knows that this small sound... will break him. He'll lose his mind. What's he gonna do? He's up in space, alone, in a space closet. He's got 25 days left to go... with this sound. So the cosmonaut decides... the only way to save his sanity... is to fall in love with this sound. So he closes his eyes... and he goes into his imagination, and then he opens them. He doesn't hear ticking anymore. He hears music. And he spends the sailing through space in total bliss... and peace.

<u>First Man</u>

Neil Armstrong: Well, we need to fail. We need to fail down here, so we don't fail up there.

Deke Slayton: The Soviets have beaten us at every single major space accomplishment. Our program couldn't compete. So we've chosen to focus on a job so difficult, requiring so many technological developments, that the Russians are going to have to start from scratch, as will we.

Pete Conrad: Neil, I was sorry to hear about your daughter.

Neil Armstrong: I'm sorry, is there a question?

Pete Conrad: What I mean is, do you think it will have an effect?

Neil Armstrong: I think it would be unreasonable to assume that it wouldn't have some effect.

Deke Slayton: Jan, you have to trust us. We've got this under control.

Janet Armstrong: No, you don't. All these protocols and procedures to make it seem like you have it under control. But you're a bunch of boys making models out of balsa wood. You don't have anything under control!

Deke Slayton: Neil, we had a problem with the plugs-out test.

Neil Armstrong: Well, that's why we have tests, right? We'll figure it out.

Reporter: Neil, if it does turn out, you'll go down in history. What kind of thoughts do you have about that when the thought hits you, “Uh, gosh, suppose that flight’s successful…”

Neil Armstrong: We’re planning on that flight being successful.

<u>Interstellar</u>

Brand: We're gonna be spending a lot of time together.

Cooper: We should learn to talk.

Brand: And when not to?

My comment: TARS is a robot in the movie.

Cooper: Hey TARS, what's your honesty parameter?

TARS: 90 percent.

Cooper: 90 percent?

TARS: Absolute honesty isn't always the most diplomatic nor the safest form of communication with emotional beings.

Cooper: Okay, 90 percent it is.

Brand: We need the bravest humans to finds us a new home.

Cooper: But the nearest star is over thousand years away.

Doyle: Hence the bravery.

Cooper: You're a scientist, Brand.

Brand: So listen to me when I say love isn't something that we invented. It's observable. Powerful. It has to mean something.

Cooper: Love has meaning, yes. Social utility, social bonding, child rearing...

Brand: We love people who have died. Where's the social utility in that?

Cooper: None.

Brand: Maybe it means something more - something we can't yet understand. Maybe it's some evidence, some artifact of a higher dimension that we can't consciously perceive. I'm drawn across the universe to someone I haven't seen in a decade who I know is probably dead. Love is the one thing that we're capable of perceiving that transcends dimensions of time and space. Maybe we should trust that, even if we can't understand it. All right, Cooper. Yes, the tiniest possibility of seeing Wolf again excites me. That doesn't mean I'm wrong.

Dr. Mann: You have attachments. But even without a family, I can promise you that...that yearning to be with other people is powerful. That emotion is at the foundation of what makes us human. It's not to be taken lightly.

Dr. Mann: You know why we couldn't just send machines on these missions, don't you, Cooper? A machine doesn't improvise well, because you can't program the fear of death. Our survival instinct is our single greatest source of inspiration. Take you, for example; a father, with a survival instinct that extends to your kids. What does research tell us is the last thing you're gonna see before you die? Your children. Their faces. At the moment of death, your mind is gonna push a little bit harder to survive. For them.

Cloud Atlas

Choice quotes of Sonmi~451:

All revolutions are, until they happen, then they are historical inevitabilities.

Knowledge is a mirror, and for the first time in my life, I was allowed to see who I was, and who I might become.

To be is to be perceived. And so to know thyself is only possible through the eyes of the other. The nature of our immortal lives is in the consequences of our words and deeds that go on and are pushing themselves throughout all time. Our lives are not our own. We are bound to others, past and present, and by each crime and every kindness, we birth our future.

Truth is singular. Its 'versions' are mistruths.

Choice quotes of Isaac Sachs:

Belief, like fear or love, is a force to be understood as we understand the theory of relativity and principals of uncertainty. Phenomena that determine the course of our lives. Yesterday, my life was headed in one direction. Today, it is headed in another. Yesterday, I believe I would never have done what I did today. These forces that often remake time and space, that can shape and alter who we imagine ourselves to be, begin long before we are born and continue after we perish. Our lives and our choices, like quantum trajectories, are understood moment to moment. That each point of intersection, each encounter, suggests a new potential direction.

Proposition, I have fallen in love with Luisa Rey. Is this possible? I just met her and yet, I feel like something important has happened to me.

Choice quote of Robert Frobisher:

I know that separation is an illusion. My life extends far beyond the limitations of me.

Choice quote from Adam Ewing:

If God created the world, how do we know what things we can change, and what things must remain sacred and inviolable?

Haskell Moore: There is a natural order to this world, and those who try to upend it do not fare well. This movement will never survive; if you join them you and your entire family will be shunned. At best, you will exist at pariah to be spat at and beaten; at worst to be lynched or crucified. And for what? No matter what you do it will never amount to anything more than a single drop in a limitless ocean.

Adam Ewing: What is an ocean but a multitude of drops?

Javier Gomes: What are you reading?

Luisa Rey: Old letters.

Javier: Why do you keep reading them?

Luisa Rey: I don't know. Just trying to understand something.

Javier: What?

Luisa Rey: Why we keep making the same mistakes... over and over.

Archivist: The report said Commander Chang was killed in the assault.

Sonmi-451: That is correct.

Archivist: Would you say that you loved him?

Sonmi-451: Yes, I do.

Archivist: Do you mean you are still in love with him?

Sonmi-451: I mean that I will always be.

Archivist: In your revelation, you spoke of the consequences of an individual's life rippling throughout eternity. Does this mean you believe in afterlife? Of a heaven or hell?

Sonmi-451: I believe death is only a door; when it closes, another opens. If I care to imagine heaven, I would imagine a door opening. And behind it, I would find him there, waiting for me.

Archivist: If I may ask one last question. You had to know this union scheme was doomed to fail.

Sonmi-451: Yes.

Archivist: Then why did you agree to it?

Sonmi-451: This is what General Apis asked of me.

Archivist: What? To be executed?

Sonmi-451: If I had remained invisible, the truth would have stayed hidden. I couldn't allow that.

Archivist: And what if no one believes this truth?

Sonmi-451: Someone already does.

<u>X-Men: Days of Future Past</u>

Prof Charles Xavier: Countless choices define our fate: each choice, each moment, a moment in the ripple of time. Enough ripple, and you change the tide...for the future is never truly set.

Push

Cassie Holmes: Right now, the future I see doesn't look so great. The good news is, the future is always changing, in the largest of ways, by the smallest of things. They've been winning a lot of battles. Now it's our turn to win the war.

The Lost City of Z

In the movie, the lead character Percy Fawcett and his son are captured by a native tribe and face the possibility of death. Percy, seeing his son trembling in fear, tries to assure his son: "Be brave. Nothing will happen to us that is not our destiny."

Robocop (2014)

Background: In this futuristic movie, Alex Murphy a cop is critically injured in the line of duty. A multinational conglomerate,

OmniCorp, seizes the opportunity and makes a part-man, part-robot police officer out of Murphy. In the dialogue that follows, the doctor explains how this Robocop (Murphy) actually works.

Dr. Dennett Norton: His software is faster. His hardware is stronger. He's a better machine.

Liz Kline: But you said humans hesitate.

Dr. Dennett Norton: Only when they're making decisions.

Liz Kline: He's not making decisions?

Dr. Dennett Norton: Well, yes and no. In his everyday life, man rules over the machine; Alex makes his own decisions. Now, when he engages in battle, the visor comes down and the software takes over, then the... the machine does everything. Alex is a... he's a passenger, just along for the ride.

Liz Kline: But if the machine is in control, then how is Murphy accountable? Who's pulling the trigger?

Dr. Dennett Norton: When the machine fights, the system releases signals into Alex's brain making him think he's doing what our computers are actually doing. I mean, Alex believes right now he is in control, but he's not. It... it's the illusion of free will.

Mindwalk

What does self-maintaining mean? Well, it means that a living system, although depending on its environment, is not determined by it. Take the yellow fields of rye around the French island of Mont St. Michel. With all the rain here, those fields should be green all year round, but every summer they turn yellow. Why? Well, to use a metaphor, each plant "remembers" that it originated in the hot and dry climate of southern Asia; it remembers, and not even a dramatically different climate can change its inner workings. Self-maintaining, self-organizing.

How to Get Away With Murder (2014 TV Series)

Three steps to get away with murder:

1. Discredit the witness.

2. Find a new suspect.

3. Bury the evidence.

Homeland (TV series)

In one episode, the lead character Carrie Mathison breaks up a pill and inhales it through the nose using a straw. I guess she did this to have a quicker effect. Snorting drugs into the nose, or nasal insufflation, causes a much faster onset of effect than ingestion, as it is absorbed quickly into the bloodstream via the soft tissue in the nasal cavity.

Midnight Special

The main characters in the movie needed to drive at night without been noticed. So the driver turned off the headlights and drove with night vision goggles.

Battleship

I learned from the movie:

-How to get information on your enemy position without a radar. By tracking water displacement.

-How to track water displacement. The tsunami buoys that surrounds the islands transmit displacement data. When a buoy gets hit by a wave, it transmits a signal displayed via NOAA data.

<u>Sherlock (BBC TV Series)</u>

Three points I gleaned:

1) Everyone has a use, and it is up to us to recognize the value. Sherlock has eyes and ears all over the city. He achieves this via The Homeless Network - a network of homeless people in London he set up. He uses this network as a source of information on cases he is working on, by paying them for the information. In fact, he even brags to a detective that he can get information faster than even the police can. Sherlock certainly makes good use of resources that people look down upon.

2) Charles Augustus Magnussen blackmails key political figures by having information

they don't want to be known publicly. When a parliamentary committee member enlists Sherlock's help to recover the information Magnussen has on her, Sherlock deduces that the villain does not hold this information in a computer. Computers can be hacked. So Magnussen is most likely to physically hold it in a vault. Only towards the end it is revealed that the information resides only in Magnussen's "mind palace." In the post-apocalyptic film The Book of Eli, the hero apparently holds the only remaining copy of the Bible. The 'bad guys' want it, so they pursue the hero and finally manage to secure it. They realize later that there is nothing printed, because it is in Braille. As the film ends, Eli dictates the entire King James Bible from memory. Yes, what we have within ourselves can outwit a villain, survive a holocaust and cannot be hacked.

3) There are such things as coincidences. Seemingly unrelated cases connect the dots for Sherlock.

<u>World War Z</u>

Background: Dr. Andrew Fassbach is a virologist.

Dr. Andrew Fassbach: Mother Nature is a serial killer; no one's better or more creative. Like all serial killers, she can't help the urge to wanna get caught -- what good were all the brilliant crimes if no one takes credit? So she leaves crumbs. Now the hard part, where you spend a decade at school, is seeing the crumbs for the clues they are. Sometimes the thing you thought was the most brutal aspect of the virus turns out to be the chink in its armor. And she loves disguising her weaknesses as strengths.

Two other notes I made from this movie:

1) There is a scene where the swarms of zombies scale the wall into Jerusalem. I believe this depicts a biological phenomenon called self-organization where individual components follow a few simple rules, but in totality, they create a larger structure that has the appearance of design. For example, schools of fish and flocks of birds make sudden movements together in harmony. A fish, a bird or a zombie (as in

this movie), is merely following a simple cue in the environment without any grasp of a grand plan. Despite that, it is possible for a larger and effective structure to emerge. What if that actually applies to us humans too? We are all acting out, based on certain impulses and self-interest to external stimuli. Even though, at times it may look chaotic or unpleasant, what if there is a grand plan that we may never fully appreciate during our lifetime? Perhaps life is not a series of random meaningless episodes?

2) In the movie, the protagonist injects himself with a less lethal virus to make himself 'invisible' to the zombies. In nature, we see prey animal employing various defense mechanisms. For example, possums emit fluid that produces a foul smell and tricks its predators into thinking that it is dead.

<u>The Walking Dead</u>

Though this is a fictional TV series and zombies do not exist for now, I wonder how is it that the zombies can go on without food and sleep for so long. One possible explanation is that they don't have fear, anxiety and a lot of other emotions that drain a normal human being's energy. The zombies are restricted to a few sets of actions and reactions that require no thinking, hence the brain does not burn as many calories.

Luther

Background: Luther, a Detective Chief Inspector (DCI), questions Alice, a suspect.

DCI Luther: No, I wouldn't be so foolish. But I will tell you this, Alice. You can revel in your brilliance for as long as you like, but people slip up. Happens time and time again.

Alice Morgan: Well, that's just faulty logic postulated on imperfect data collection. What if you only catch people who make mistakes? That would skew the figures, wouldn't it?

DCI John Luther: There was no evidence of an intruder.

Alice Morgan: But absence of evidence isn't evidence of absence.

Alice Morgan: Did they make me a freak? Yes. Did I hate them? Absolutely. Did I kill them? No.

DCI John Luther: Can you prove that?

Alice Morgan: I can't prove a negative. Can't be done.

DCI John Luther: I love to talk about nothing. It's the only thing I know anything about.

<u>Total Recall (2012)</u>

Doug Quaid: I want to remember.

Matthias: Why?

Doug Quaid: So I can be myself, be who I was.

Matthias: It is each man's quest to find out who he truly is, but the answer to that lies in the present, not in the past. As it is for all of us.

Doug Quaid: But the past tells us who we've become.

Matthias: The past is a construct of the mind. It blinds us. It fools us into believing it. But the heart wants to live in the present. Look there. You'll find your answer.

<u>Bridge Of Spies</u>

James Donovan: You don't look alarmed.
Rudolf Abel: Is that gonna help?

Rudolf Abel: Well, the boss isn't always right… But he is always the boss.

James Donovan: It doesn't matter what others think. You know what you did.

My comment: James tells that to Rudolf Abel as Abel was concerned that his countrymen will think he broke under pressure.

Flash of Genius

This movie is based on a real American entrepreneur, Robert Kearns.

Robert Kearns: Good morning, everybody. I want to welcome you all to the first day of the quarter for Applied Electrical Engineering. My name is Dr. Robert Kearns and I'd like to start by talking to you about ethics. I can't think of a job or a career where the understanding of ethics is more important than engineering. Who designed the artificial aortic heart valve?

An engineer did that. And who designed the gas chambers at Auschwitz?

An engineer did that, too. One man was responsible for helping save tens of thousands of lives, another man helped kill millions. Now, I don't know what any of you are gonna end up doing in your lives, but I can guarantee you that there will come a day where you have a decision to make, and it won't be as easy as deciding between a heart valve and a gas chamber.

Everything we do in this classroom ultimately comes back to that notion.

Jobs

Steve Wozniak to Steve Jobs: Not everyone has an agenda, Steve. It's about yourself. You're the beginning and the end of your own world and it's gotta be sad and lonely.

Liberator

Maestro to Simon Bolivar: You are so poor that the only thing you have is money.

Daredevil season 1, episode 7

Two quotes from the character, Stick:

Anger is a spark – good. Rage is a wildfire that is out of control, therefore useless.

Surrounding yourself with soft stuff isn't life it's death.

We Bought a Zoo

Benjamin Mee: You know, sometimes all you need is twenty seconds of insane courage. Just literally twenty seconds of just embarrassing bravery. And I promise you, something great will come of it.

Green Lantern

Will power within us allows us to create whatever we can imagine. The earthling Hal Jordon was chosen by the ring not because he was devoid of fear, but rather because he had the ability to overcome great fear. Fear weakens our willpower, and anger will make it unfocused. A Green Lantern needs to be focused.

The Amazing Spiderman 2

Gwen Stacy's Valedictorian Speech:

I know that we all think we're immortal; we're supposed to feel that way, we're graduating. The future is and should be bright, but, like our brief four years in high school, what makes life valuable is that it doesn't last forever; what makes it precious is that it ends. I know that now more than ever. And I say it today of all days to remind us that time is luck. So don't waste it living someone else's life; make yours count for something. Fight for what matters to you, no matter what. Because even if you fall short, what better way is there to live?

It's easy to feel hopeful on a beautiful day like today, but there will be dark days ahead of us, too, and there'll be days where you feel all alone, and that's when hope is needed most. Keep it alive. No matter how buried it gets, or lost you feel, you must promise me, that you will hold on to hope and keep it alive. We have to be greater than what we suffer. My wish for you is to become hope. People need that.

I know it feels like we're saying goodbye, but we will carry a piece of each other into everything that we do next, to remind us of who we are, and of who we're meant to be. I've had a great four years with you, and I'll miss you all very much.

Hellboy

Agent John Myers' monologue: What makes a man a man, a friend once wondered. Is it his origins, the way he comes to life? I don't think so. It's the choices he makes; not how he starts things, but how he decides to end things.

Made in United States
Orlando, FL
04 June 2024

47533941R00125